# I Want to Get Married!

One Wannabe Bride's
Misadventures with Handsome
Houdinis, Technicolor Grooms,
Morality Police, and Other
Mr. Not-Quite-Rights

EMERGING VOICES FROM THE MIDDLE EAST

*Series Editor*
Tarek El-Ariss

*Editorial Committee*
M. R. Ghanoonparvar *&* Karen Grumberg

# I Want to Get Married!

One Wannabe Bride's Misadventures with Handsome Houdinis, Technicolor Grooms, Morality Police, and Other Mr. Not-Quite-Rights

## BY GHADA ABDEL AAL

### TRANSLATED BY NORA ELTAHAWY

The Center for Middle Eastern Studies
The University of Texas at Austin

Cover art: © iStockphoto, Veronica Davies
Cover and text design: Kristi Shuey
Editor: Wendy E. Moore

Library of Congress Control Number: 2010934842
ISBN: 978-0-292-72397-9

Originally published in Arabic as *Ayza Atgawez*.
© Ghada Abdel Aal 2007
© Dar El Shorouk 2007

# Table of Contents

# INTRODUCTION:
## EMERGING VOICES FROM THE MIDDLE EAST

In this new millennium, the Middle East is witnessing an unprecedented literary revolution, with new voices ushering in new articulations of identity, social models, and literary genres. The Center for Middle Eastern Studies at the University of Texas at Austin, with its long and prestigious tradition of publishing Arabic, Persian, Turkish, and Hebrew fiction in translation, is proud to present these daring and innovative works in a series entitled Emerging Voices from the Middle East. By focusing on new authors who began publishing in the twenty-first century, this series will introduce readers to writers who are at the cutting edge of Middle Eastern culture.

The broad scope of this series is intended to reflect the wide spectrum of expression that has come into being since the turn of the millennium. For example, the works created by one important contingent of this new generation of authors emerge from spaces at the intersection of the novel and the blog, poetry and hip-hop, and native language and English, and are full of references to classical and modern Middle Eastern literatures, Hollywood films and TV series, and the Internet. These authors are flaunting their new knowledge and technological abilities, unapologetically incorporating popular culture into their literary works. They are coming into writing from the world of blogging and scriptwriting, mixing languages and traditions. On the other hand, this diverse generation also includes authors who write from within a localized context and who are developing new modes of confronting the political and ideological concerns that preoccupied previous literary generations. Some do so by introducing humor where seriousness reigned; others reject their contemporaries' media-language in favor of a new formalism. The wide range of the aesthetic and theoretical manifestations of this writing captures a new Middle Eastern experience that requires attention and translation.

These new authors, many of whom were born in the 1970s and 1980s, grew up watching Hollywood films and American sitcoms, and some went back and forth between the Middle East and the West or the Gulf countries. They are comfortable with the Internet, cell phones, and all that the information age has made possible in terms of communication and digitization. This generation relates to English not as a foreign language, but as the language that is constitutive of their cultural landscape. These emerging voices are breaking the boundaries of language and literature by introducing a new way of seeing and representing the world around them. Their works move beyond the neatly organized binary oppositions of East and West, religiosity and secularism, tradition and modernity, and even Arab and Jew. Using a multiplicity of languages and voices, these authors are producing multilayered structures that bring into literature the experience of globalized subjects. Exposing and reflecting new social and political realities, many of these works are being turned into films and TV series with great commercial success, complicating the relation between literature and media, high art, and popular culture.

As they challenge the requirements of literary canons and cultural models established by state institutions, these new authors are reproducing the experience of a subject who is fundamentally distrustful of—or altogether indifferent to—ideology and grand causes, including revolution, nationalism, and the rhetoric of loss and mourning. This literature is no longer in the service of governments and political ideals; it reflects instead the aspirations of a new generation seeking to define itself and engage others across cultural, political, and linguistic spaces. Urban experiences, foreign settings, and colloquial languages and dialects are used to represent a reality often masked by political discourse, cultural censorship, and miscommunication.

Irreverent, bold, and bitingly humorous, Ghada Abdel Aal's (b. 1978) *I Want to Get Married!* (originally published in Arabic in 2008) is representative of the contingent of new authors who, while writing about their personal experiences in a complex cultural landscape, are employing a familiar if not at times casual language, free of artifice and traditional complexities. Their works have introduced many innovations into the literary text, including stream of consciousness and fragmented narratives, the didactic genre of the interview, and the preponderance of English words and such e-writing acronyms as "lol" and "@." They deal with questions of sexuality, religious extremism, and youth culture, addressing a reading public eager to explore issues relevant to its daily life. Some works are published under pen names, reflecting the anonymity of bloggers, but also employing pre-modern narrative structures like that in *Thousand and One Nights*. With excessive use of "!!!" "…" and "???," these works have masterfully incorporated the language of affects, from anger and rebellion to happiness and pleasure. This serves to directly address the reader, inviting him/her to actively engage the work and experience rather than simply understand its meaning.

In *I Want to Get Married!*, originally a blog, a young single Egyptian woman satirizes arranged marriages in Egypt. She describes failed attempts to meet "Mr. Right" in the traditional way, exposing in the process the hypocrisy of social mores and the prevailing economic forces. A pharmacist by training, Abdel Aal provides a colorful set of characters such as Auntie-Body the matchmaker; the thief who declares his marital intentions in order to mug Bride (Abdel Aal); the would-be groom who can only watch and react to a soccer game on TV while visiting his potential in-laws; and the suitor who is presented as a successful professional working in the oil-rich Gulf countries, while in fact he is a poor employee in a remote provincial town in Egypt.

Abdel Aal exposes the gender relations involved in such rituals, thereby critiquing parents' desperateness to see their daughter married off and eligible bachelors acting like immature teenagers. She humorously describes her various encounters with suitors, highlighting the effects of a fluctuating social and economic situation on marriage and romance. Combining Egyptian slang with English and French expressions interspersed throughout, Abdel Aal denounces, lampoons, and riles. Her work goes back and forth between narrating conversations and incidents, sustaining a fast pace that makes the book a successful adaptation of a popular blog.

*I Want to Get Married!*'s style and publication history positions it at the forefront of a new literary genre in the Middle East. Produced at the intersection of the virtual and the material, the blog and the novel, this work's originality and popularity with a young generation of Egyptian readers has earned it critical recognition both in the Middle East and abroad. Countless articles and interviews with the author appeared in local newspapers as well as Western media outlets. Furthermore, due to its humor and episodic nature, the work is now a TV series starring Egypt's Hend Sabri.

From the blog to the book and now the TV series, the production trajectory of *I Want to Get Married!* across media constitutes an important articulation of new writing coming out of the Middle East today. Translated by Nora Eltahawy, this work is the first publication in the series Emerging Voices from the Middle East. In a landscape saturated with stereotypical representations of the other, this series showcases new voices and provides a window into a complex cultural space, thereby facilitating communication and promoting dialogue across national and linguistic boundaries.

Tarek El-Ariss
Series Editor

Since it was started in 2006, Ghada Abdel Aal's blog, I Want
to Get Married!, has received over 500,000 hits and has been
featured in a slew of regional and international media outlets,
including *Arab News*, *The Washington Post*, the *Los Angeles Times*,
the BBC, and *The Independent*. First published in 2008 by the
Egyptian publishing house Dar El-Shorouk, the blog-turned-
book has since become a best seller and, aside from English, has
been translated into Italian, German, and Dutch. In August
2010, the sitcom inspired by I Want to Get Married! made its
small-screen debut during Ramadan, the most popular and
competitive season for TV viewership in the Middle East.

   The popularity reflected in these accomplishments is perhaps
best explained when, on her Blogspot profile, Abdel Aal describes
herself as representing fifteen million Egyptian women between
the ages of twenty-five and thirty-five pressured by their society
into getting married and blamed when they fail to do so. Although
sociologists and journalists have long discussed such pressures
in the Egyptian media, Abdel Aal's writing signifies one of the
earliest attempts by her generation to voice its own concerns on the
matter and to do so through a medium that is populated heavily by
the country's youth. That the voice to achieve this is both female
and decidedly personal marks a departure from stoic discussions
led by older Egyptian professionals and has become the focal
point of the media attention received by I Want to Get Married!
In a culture that likes to use the saying "Homes are made of
secrets," Abdel Aal has opened the door to hers, challenging the
pressure traditionally placed on women to keep silent about such
issues within the Middle East, and defying Western onlookers'
expectations of the exclusive performance of that traditionalism.

   The importance of Abdel Aal's gender and her insistence on
representing the women of her country notwithstanding, I Want
to Get Married! has proven itself to be extremely popular with
Egyptian men as well. Despite what the disparaging commentator

we meet in one chapter of the book may believe, Abdel Aal is not speaking for old maids but is, rather, astutely aware of the consequences that arise due to the psychological and financial pressure placed on women and men, respectively. In Egypt the pressure to marry is combined with a fluctuating unemployment rate, an expensive and dwindling rental market, and average incomes that place one fifth or more of the population under the poverty line. With the exception of young couples whose parents can afford to finance their marriages, such conditions make the traditional costs associated with getting married in Egypt—Abdel Aal's infamous furniture, the down payment for an apartment, wedding jewelry, and a wedding—unfeasible for a significant number of young people.

While many turn to the *'urfi*, or undocumented, marriages satirized in I Want to Get Married!, others, like Abdel Aal herself, take to the Internet. Aided partly by the popularity of Internet cafes that facilitate logging on for a few pounds an hour, Egypt boasts the highest number of bloggers and subscribers to social networking sites in the Middle East. Where Abdel Aal's blog is concerned, this ease of access has, along with the societal particularities described above, lent I Want to Get Married! a wide and overwhelmingly sympathetic readership base. Abdel Aal maintains that it is her readers who first urged her to publish her blog as a book and to explore the possibility of creating a television show. Averaging hundreds of comments per post, the electronic version of I Want to Get Married! serves as a forum both for its author and for its readers, who leave Abdel Aal everything from personal analyses of delayed marriage in Egypt, to criticism of governmental, economic, or parental policies, to one male reader's tongue-in-cheek reminder that both men and women are in the same sinking ship.

Though it may seem to be sinking quickly, the ship Abdel Aal occupies with her peers is one that she illustrates in a dizzying combination of dialects, languages, and pop culture references. In the course of her writing, Abdel Aal offsets the Egyptian dialect she uses in the majority of the work, and which she manipulates alternately into lighthearted satire or angry speechifying, with religious citations, Arab cultural references, Modern Standard Arabic, transliterated English, and American celebrity culture. While this combination is far from unusual in a country exposed equally to the lived realities of the Middle East and the televised ones of the West, it is one that offers a particular challenge in translation. Where Abdel Aal is free to insert two versions of Arabic into her writing—the colloquial Egyptian dialect and the decidedly more formal Modern Standard Arabic—my translation has had to reflect the change in dialect through manipulations of tone. Where Abdel Aal uses Modern Standard Arabic, traditionally associated with classicism, highbrow literature, and official reports—and used by Abdel Aal to mock all three—I reflect the change through highly verbose prose that is both ridiculous and frequently difficult to understand. Far less systematic is my approach to the transliterated English Abdel Aal incorporates. While, in one instance, I borrow from Humphrey Davies's tactic of using French to reflect the transliteration, a method that maintains a similar class-based commentary in English, I seamlessly incorporate the transliterations in other cases where I believe the meaning to be unaffected. In the case of both Auntie-Body's *shobbing* and Habby Falantine, I deliberately inscribe the words the way they would have been pronounced by the targets of Abdel Aal's satire. Native speakers of a language that contains no distinction between the letters *b* and *p*, Egyptians frequently confuse the two letters when speaking English and, in both cases where I make use of this, I find the sarcasm to be heightened by the confusion in pronunciation. Finally, I have kept all of the direct cultural references (names of actors, references to Islamic or Egyptian celebrations, etc....) as they are in the Arabic version and have changed only small expressions that work better in their nearest American cultural approximations than in direct translation. Throughout the process, the aim was to present the particularities of Abdel Aal's story free of exoticizing and of a literalness of language that would have overburdened the translation with footnotes. In finding this balance, I was helped greatly by Tarek El-Ariss, to whom I also owe Auntie-Body's name in English, and by Wendy Moore, who let me keep Nancy Agram's name the way it would be pronounced by an Egyptian. Any mistakes are mine alone.

# I Want to Get Married!

One Wannabe Bride's Misadventures with Handsome Houdinis, Technicolor Grooms, Morality Police, and Other Mr. Not-Quite-Rights

# The Beginning of the Story

Say your *bismillahs* and stick with me step by step.* First off, let's just agree that this whole marriage, and suitors, and marrying late business is really sensitive. It's also hard to find anyone who talks about it honestly. Especially girls. Because girls who talk about this honestly are either seen as crass and badly raised, or as obsessed with getting married. Either that or as old maids who can't find anyone to marry them. That's why you find so many girls saying things like:

—"Marriage schmarriage! What did married people ever get that was so great?!"

—"I live like a princess in my parents' house—what would make me go tough it out with someone I don't know? I'm not thinking about marriage at all these days. Not till I'm done building my future."

And that one line used to death in all Arabic movies: "Not till I achieve self-realization." . . . I have no idea what this "self" deal is and how anyone's supposed to go about realizing it.

There may be a lot of girls out there who are ambitious about what they study and about their jobs, but I bet you that there isn't a single one of them whose first ambition isn't to be a wife, at the very least because it's the only way to be a mother.

Now we need to agree on another key point: there are more women in Egypt than men.

That's an indisputable fact. Never you mind the government statistics that tell you the figures are the same, because those

*An abbreviation of *bismillah al-rahman al-rahim*, which translates to "In the name of God, the Compassionate, the Merciful"; the phrase begins each chapter of the Qur'an and, traditionally, is used by Muslims when embarking on new ventures.

statistics are just like the weather reports on the news every night. Everyone could be swearing on their mothers' lives that the temperature has to be higher than 48°C and they'll never report anything higher than 38°C. My dad's friend says they're not allowed to announce anything higher than 42°C. So that the tourism industry doesn't suffer a blow and the tourists don't run away.

The female-male ratio thing has been messed around with, too. Why are there more girls?

I'll tell you.

The thing is that women keep having kids until they have a boy. You'll find a ton of families out there who are like that . . . four girls and a boy . . . five girls and a boy . . . six girls and a boy, etc. . . . A woman will keep popping kids out so that her moron husband can have a son. What's he going to do with that son that's so important? No idea. So at the end of the day, the kid becomes a good-for-nothing loser who's spoiled rotten and who'll blow through everything his parents have . . . Anyway, that's a whole other issue. But anyone who's studying or has studied at any Egyptian university will have noticed that there are more girls on campuses than boys. At my university, for instance, two-thirds of the students were girls and only a third were boys—double the amount of girls.

And another thing—men have become full of themselves and act like they're too good for all of womankind (may their eyes and health be stricken, amen!), and so you'll find men sitting around with their mothers, laying their ground rules:

"She has to be fair skinned, with brown hair and hazel eyes, and she has to look like Nelly Karim." Damn you all, I say! Maybe you should take a look at yourself in the mirror first, buddy! Or, you know what? Never mind looks—they say the only thing that can shame a man is his wallet. Well, go ahead and splurge, then, Mister, and bring along a teeny box of candy when you visit. But no . . . the idiot and his mommy will go check out a poor bride whose parents have spent a ton on her, and who've lavishly financed the "getting-to-know-you" meeting, and he'll walk in empty-handed. The girl could have absolutely nothing wrong with her, and they'll say, "No, she doesn't really look like Nelly Karim . . . she's more of a Naglaa Fathy, who's really not my type."* You'd think it was Hussein Fahmy trying to find a bride, I swear to God.†

Oh, and weddings—they're a JOKE. A long time ago you'd see a girl in an Arabic movie walking into a wedding, dressed all chic-like, and a bunch of guys would gather around her, looking like they wanted to eat her all up, and there would be no way she'd leave that wedding without a man to marry. Now, it's the same gatherings, but the tables are turned—every mother sits around with her daughters watching the young men, and woe be to he who passes by them! "Tarek, how *are* you, boy?! Aren't you going to come say hello to your cousins and see how pretty they've gotten?!" "I'm not Tarek, Tante, and I'm pretty sure you're not my aunt." "Oh, really? You have to forgive me, sweetheart, my vision isn't what it used to be. But why don't you come introduce yourself anyway? Maybe God will smile down on you and your luck will change with us!"

So of course, either the guy bolts out of there, or one of his friends notices the trap he's fallen into and saves him by pretending someone needs him.

Obviously, this is all in addition to how girls twirl around a bride on the dance floor so that they can be on display to everyone in the ballroom from all angles. And when the twirling's done, they'll shove each other or pretend to adjust the

---

*Egyptian actresses known for their good looks.
†Egyptian actor known for his aristocratic background and good looks.

bride's gown or veil so that they get on camera. And they'll try to show up in as many pictures as possible because, that way, maybe they'll catch someone's eye and he'll swoop in and pluck them out of the single girls' world.

You're not supposed to laugh at all this, by the way. Those girls are poor souls, I swear. A long time ago, all a girl had to do was have self-respect and sit around in her parents' house waiting for The One, who, more often than not, would be someone her parents chose anyway.

Now the ball's in the girls' court, which means they have to get out there and work at it and go to weddings and visit friends because the responsibility of finding a mate has been hurled solely on their shoulders. I know lots of families who'll raise hell with their daughters so that they'll go out and work at it, because otherwise they may never get married. And on the flip side, a lot of the time society—especially outside of Cairo and Alexandria—will be merciless toward girls who go out with men so that they can get to know them and then maybe decide to make a commitment. Not to mention the fact that men themselves will turn the women down, saying they want to marry someone "pure" who's never gone out with another guy or spoken to one.

So, seriously now, what's a girl supposed to do?! All of this is in addition to the stopwatch that starts counting down as soon as girls graduate from college. So they can consider themselves old maids if they're not engaged two or three years after they graduate.

Personally, I started feeling like a spinster as soon as I hit twenty-three. So what do we do?

Honestly, the damn society we live in that rates girls according to the marriages they land, and that values women who get married super quick and that thinks there must be something wrong with the ones who don't, and that says, on the other hand, that it's a man's right to choose and be picky and that players are open-minded men of the world, and that sees nothing wrong with men getting married anytime after forty, even if it's to an eighteen-year-old . . . that society is just UNFAIR and cruel!

So that's why I, "Bride" (I'm using English here so people think I'm classy), have decided to write about this and explain the situation from all possible angles so that people who don't understand can get it, and so that people who don't know can find out—that girls are poor little things, that the pressure they're under gets worse every day, and that people judge them for something in which they have no hand.

So stick with me and I'll tell you about each of the many losers who's proposed to me. So you can see just how much we have to put up with . . .

## Why Do I Want to Get Married?
### 10–15 Reasons (But don't count on me)

Sometimes I'll sit and wonder: Why do I even want to get married in the first place? I'm pretty great just the way I am: I'm a respected pharmacist, I make (actually, never mind how much I make, in case you laugh at me) . . . I'm alive, I eat, I drink, I sleep, I go out, I have fun, I go to the movies, I watch TV like I can't bear to look away . . . So where's the problem?!

Other times, though, I feel like there are lots of reasons why I'd want to get married. I'm sure that girls who lead all kinds of different lives feel the same way too.

One girl, for example, might say: "I want to get married so that I can have kids."

A second might say: "I want to get married so people don't call me an old maid."

A third might say: "I want to get married so I can let loose and be free!" (She's an idiot, but what can you do?)

A fourth might say: "I want to get married so I can give birth to an Arab hero, the next Saladin." (Niiiiice one! I guess it's possible.)

Now *I* have a completely different set of reasons. Nothing Big and Important like the reasons I just listed (Or like, say, that it's within my rights to want to get married. That it's not shameful or wrong). It's the small things that matter to me. Because, like Mervat Amin says in *And the Train of Life Has Passed, My Child* (take the one after it that leaves at a quarter to four), "small things give life its flavor." . . . That movie was so deep.

Anyway, here are 10–15 moments when I feel like I need a husband:

1. When the gas cylinder runs out and needs to be changed. This is, of course, one of a husband's main household duties.
2. When I see a roach in the house and I freak out and I can't kill it . . . God, it would be a disaster if the person I end up marrying is scared of roaches too.
3. When it's lunchtime and Mama and Baba eat the drumsticks and leave the chicken breast for me. Even if my husband doesn't like the breast either, chickens have two drumsticks for two people!
4. When I take the mattresses up to the roof to air them out. When I'm married, I can pretend that I need my husband to help out just a teeny bit, then make him carry the whole load.
5. At the movies when they separate the singles from the families at the entrances. I mean, they get to be married AND they get to go to the cinema together?! How unfair is that?!*

*In smaller Egyptian cities, cinemas often dedicate one side of the theater to families and the other to single men. Single women will sit in either section depending on local custom.

6. When it's time to ride the microbus. I'm sure a husband would protect me from all the bumps and gropes . . . if he's not busy groping the girl next to him, that is.

7. When I get home after I've fought with my boss and I need to take all my rage out on someone. If I yelled at my mom or dad . . . well, I'd go to hell. But with a husband, it's okay.

8. When one of my married friends gets a phone call from her husband telling her that she's forgotten the food on the stove and that the apartment's on fire . . . why can't I have my own apartment that can catch on fire too?!

9. When I'm alone in bed at night (Hey! No pervy thoughts!). At least a husband could act as a barrier to stop me from falling off the bed every night.

10. When Mama cooks something I don't like. When will I be in control of what gets cooked and when can I make whatever I want?! Anyone who doesn't like what I make can go eat at his mother's!

11. When Mama stops me from piling up junk on the balcony. When will I have my own balcony that I can fill up with junk and my own kitchen where I can store empty jam jars?!

12. When I want plums (nobody wants to get any for me these days). I could always threaten my husband and tell him that I'm pregnant and craving plums and that if he doesn't get me any the baby will come out with a plum-shaped birthmark.

13. When I'm watching a Haifa Wehbe or Nancy Agram music video and I want a man next to me so I can yell at him for checking them out.*

*Lebanese pop singers known for their provocative clothing.

14. When I write a list like this and I can't find anyone to tell me that I forgot to include a number 6. (Haha—made you look!)
15. You guys think of a number 15 because I've just reminded myself of terribly painful things and now I'm all depressed.

Anyway, there you have it: 10–15 moments when I feel like I want to get married. But there are still hundreds of other times when I feel like I'm done . . . with being single, that is.

# The First

There's a nice title for you; it's like what Anwar Wagdi used to say in *The Prince of Revenge.*\* This whole suitors business is like an Arabic movie anyway, though this first story is more like a Bollywood production . . . and a comedy at that.

A couple of weeks after I'd gone to my friend's wedding, she gave me a call to see how I was doing. I'd just heard that one of our friends had found a suitor for another one of our friends. This whole set-up business really ticks me off, by the way. There'll always be one girl who'll end up asking, "Well, why didn't you choose *me* for the set-up?!" and then she may never speak to the person doing the matchmaking ever again.

So I latched on to the friend who'd called and started to rant:

"Do you see these friends?! Why can't you do anything helpful like that?! Why do you think we married you off?! Wasn't it so that you could find us a friend of your husband's or a cousin of his or anyone remotely eligible?!"

Every few seconds my friend would try to cut me off and shut me up, but I was off and going like a rocket. Until she stopped me with a scream:

"Woman, shut *up*, my husband's listening in on the other phone to make sure you're delicate and girlie enough because he's found someone for you!"

That was when I did a complete 180 and became more delicate than the girliest girlie girl you've ever seen in your entire life:

". . . Oh, you actually believed me?! I was totally kidding around with you! You know me . . . been girlie all my life! Girlier than that new actress woman, that Mona Zaki!"

\*Egyptian actor and director (1904–1955). In the movie, Wagdi theatrically counts off the enemies he has killed using "the first," "the second," etc.

I could hear her husband trying to stifle his laughter on the other end of the line, and I could hear her gnash her teeth as she said:

"I know . . . I know. You don't have to tell *me* twice."

Anyway, we set a date for the guy to visit us. This may strike men as insignificant. What's the big deal?! He'll shower, have his mother wash his shirt and pants, make his sister iron the outfit, and put every damn person to work all for the sake of his wonderful self. But in the bride's house, in this case, in *my* house . . . CHAOS. Walls are washed, floors are mopped, rugs are beaten, banisters are waxed, glasses are polished, curtains and windows are cleaned, and after all that, after all the freaking work, the bride's expected to get herself dolled up and make her entrance, pretty and glowing.

Anyway, Mr. Precious and his family came to visit. He's a *doctor*, by the way. I glanced at him out of the corner of my eye and saw that his outfit looked like . . . oh God . . . like he'd taken all the fresh laundry off the clothesline and put everything on at once. I'm pretty sure they don't have any mirrors at their place, and it looks like his mother and sister are colorblind too. The good sir was wearing a yellow shirt . . . blue pants . . . a green sweater . . . and to top it all off . . . a tie the color of—actually, I can't even really tell what color that tie was, to be honest. Oh, and wait—brown shoes! And when he plopped down and crossed his legs, I saw that he was wearing maroon socks. Yep. I swear. I told myself that it wasn't a big deal, that they say the only thing that shames a man is his wallet. And there he was: a Technicolor groom like on a TV set, all bright and loving life. So, yes, it's true his ears looked like they weren't on speaking terms with the rest of his head, and that his teeth loved each other so very much they were crawling all over each other, but, I mean, it's all God's creation! All that matters are his mind and personality.

As soon as Baba walked in, he stood up. Nice and polite. Then his mother set off introducing him like we were on a TV show:

"Dr. Samy. Physiotherapy."

He topped his mom's intro, adding: "And I do celebrity impersonations!"

Who was this idiot?! Were we hosting a talent show, or did he think he was here to interview for a job at a nightclub?! Baba glared at him and said: "Right. Welcome. Have a seat."

Then he looked at Mama as if to ask: What is this *thing* you've brought into our house?!

I was sitting there, trying to stop myself from bursting out laughing, and the guy was still going strong, talking about his enterprises and experiences in the world of celebrity impersonations. We all looked at each other, and his mother seemed positively joyous at what her son was saying. Then, all of a sudden, he looked at the clock, then looked at Baba. My father was worried that he'd ask for my hand right then and there and that it would be awkward to have to rebuff him so quickly.

But what he said was: "Uncle . . . can I ask you something and can you give me an honest answer?"

Baba, scared: "What is it, son?!"

He said: "Does this TV work?"

Baba got all surprised and answered: "Yes, son, it works."

Suddenly, Hot Stuff got up and turned the TV on and stood, flipping through the channels, until he found one airing the Zamalek soccer game.* All the while, we were still sitting there, stunned, unable to do anything about what was happening. His mother still looked positively joyous.

Then he got loud:

"KICK IT, MAN! YES! LIKE THAT! ARRRGH! THAT REFEREE IS AN ASS SON OF A . . ." (And we were sitting right there!)

Mama tried to embarrass him politely, saying:

---

*Cairo-based soccer team. Known for its rivalry with another Cairo team, El-Ahly.

"I don't know how you follow soccer these days, Doctor. Zamalek hasn't been playing very well at all recently!"

The guy got really quiet all of a sudden. Turned to Mama in slow motion. His eyes got so red; Mama shrank in her seat. Then he let loose:

"OH NO YOU DON'T! LET ME TELL YA SOMETHING, LADY . . . ANYTHING BUT ZAMALEK! TALK ABOUT ANYONE—MY MOTHER, MY FATHER, ME PERSONALLY. BUT ZAMALEK? NO! NO! NO! YOU UNDERSTAND?! Get up, Mama! There is NO way I can be in a house where Zamalek is insulted!"

. . . You son of a crazy person! We were letting the disasters you were wearing slide, and we were looking past the moronic things you were saying, and this is what we get in return?! We all stayed glued to our seats; Baba was looking at Mama, and neither of them was able to move. I was furious at first, but then I fell off my chair laughing. Some disasters will make you cry and some will make you laugh.

The best part is when my friend came up to me the next day and asked what I thought of him. I said: "You've got to be kidding me!" I told her what had happened, and she said:

"Well, so what?! Just don't tell him you're an Ahly fan!"

When I insisted on turning the guy down, this friend of mine ditched me, and she hasn't called me since. How could I possibly reject such a great catch?!

How could I, indeed.

# I Am Not a Good-for-Nothing

Our magnificent little society has two faces. I'm not saying
anything new here, I know. Have you ever seen a family get-
together where there's a little boy and a little girl? What's
the first thing they say to the boy? "What do you want to be
when you grow up, honey?" Half of them, the bullies, will say,
"A police officer." The ones with a bit more socio-political
awareness might say, "The president." (They're the generation
of the Youth of the Future campaigns, after all.* What can you
do?) Well, what do they say to the sweet little girl then? "You
want to get married to little Hamada when you two grow up,
sweetheart? Or do you want to marry Abeh Khaled?"† And
the poor thing will stare at them dumbly and say, "I'm going to
marry my daddy!" and everyone will fall about laughing and
that's that.

Girls grow up with dolls. Brushing their hair, changing their
outfits, putting veils on them and singing like it's their wedding.
Girls in any given culture always want to play pretend the
same way: what do they act like? A bride and groom! (In kids'
understanding of the concept, naturally, not like what happens
in private schools and with undocumented marriages . . . )‡

*Initiative begun by Gamal Mubarak, the son of Egyptian president Hosni Mubarak
and the general secretary of the policy committee of the country's ruling National
Democratic Party (NDP). The campaign provided housing for low-income families and
was a means of generating support for the NDP within the country.
†Abeh is a term of respect for older male relatives. Gradually falling into disuse.
‡Undocumented, or 'urfi, marriages are never formally registered with the government
and are frequently kept secret from the couple's respective families. In a society that
discourages premarital sex, 'urfi marriages are one way young couples justify physical
intimacy without undertaking the financial costs of a "real" marriage and without
seeking the approval of either set of parents. The phenomenon has been widely
condemned by both religious scholars and sociologists.

So girls climb up the educational ladder, and every time they complete a stage, they hear, "Congratulations! I can't wait to dance at your wedding . . . May you find The One soon, sweetie." And when they ask for advice about what to major in in college, the invariable response is: "Oh, don't you worry yourself about it. Girls just end up being housewives!"

And so girls are programmed over and over again to think that the only thing that's expected of them in life is for them to get married and have children . . . But what if it doesn't happen?

Here are a bunch of different scenarios for you:

> Person 1: "How many do you have these days?"
> Person 2: "I've got two sets of gold bracelets saved."*
> P1: "No, I mean, how many kids do you have?"
> P2: "Oh. No . . . I'm still single."
> P1: "Oh, you poor thing!"

A second social class:

> P1: "How many do you have these days?"
> P2: "Degrees? I have an MA, and I'm working on my PhD."
> P1: "No, I mean, how many kids do you have?"
> P2: "Oh. No . . . I'm still single."
> P1: "Oh, you poor thing!"

And a third:

> P1: "How many do you have these days?"
> P2: "Cars? I have a 4x4 Cherokee."
> P1: "No, I mean, how many *les enfants* do you have?"

---

*Whether in the form of wedding jewelry or otherwise, gold is considered an integral part of many Middle Eastern women's savings and social standing.

P2: "Oh. *Non* . . . I'm still single."

P1: "*Mon Dieu!* Poor *chérie!*"

It's the exact same conversation, taking place on all levels of society. And no amount of success in any field can replace getting married for a Middle Eastern girl. What about the woman who can't find anyone and who's missed the train and who's obsolete, as they say? Is she useless then? Should she go set herself on fire?

Generally speaking, women aren't prepared emotionally or educationally or economically for a situation like that. Everyone tells them, "You're going to get married and that's that," and when it doesn't happen, the only person left to support them is themselves.

Now that the number of women who still haven't found anyone has hit the millions, it's time for women to learn to love themselves and to look for success wherever they can find it and live life for themselves, and not like it's the opening credits to a show that hasn't started yet.

Society needs to stop confining women solely to the role of bride. Because when things fall apart, nobody will be able to help them out after all their expectations have been shattered, after they've been taught that there's only one path to take and one path alone. Then they feel like worthless good-for-nothings, and they sit and complain, like I'm doing to you right now.

I'm saying it from the get-go: if it happens . . . if I don't get married and if I don't have children and if I can't follow society's grand plan, I will always have my independent nature and I will always have my own life and I will never be . . . a good-for-nothing.

# The Second

Didn't we decide we were going to do this Anwar Wagdi-style, already?

So look. First off, the story this time is about another one of those disasters that makes you cry and laugh at the same time. But to be really, really honest, it's me you're going to be laughing at. You'll see . . . But let me tell you, since I'm so "fragile," uh, I mean . . . such a delicate girlie girl, whose wings have been mangled (Ha! Don't you love "mangled"?) . . . please, please, don't make fun of me.

Nobody knows about this story except Mama and me. I haven't told any of my friends. So you can go ahead and brag about this great privilege to all your pals: the story of Bride's second groom . . . Extra! Extra! Read all about it!

Ahem . . . an intro: You know that feeling a woman gets when she's walking down the street and can tell that a man is checking her out? No harassment or anything, just this feeling that there's *chemistry* in the air, like the Westerners say. A lot of marriages will come about this way: a man will see a woman he likes on the street and will follow her, find out where she lives, ask around about her, and propose. My cousin followed a woman once and the girl gave him such a giant whopper of a slap her handprint was on his face for three days. So he got all happy and said that that made it obvious that she was well behaved and had been raised right, and he went ahead and asked for her hand. Yep, I swear. So, yes, it would turn out that that wouldn't be the only time she'd hit him, that she'd do it in all kinds of different situations, but the man's happy and swears by the day he met her and curses the day he met her moth—actually, never mind. She is like an aunt, after all.

Anyway, one day I was leaving my house, heading to work, when I felt some of this chemistry business I've been telling you guys about. Like there were eyes piercing the back of my head. I snuck a glance backwards and found a magnificent specimen of a man—tall and broad and high. He was carrying a briefcase and wearing a suit and tie and sunglasses. Looked like one of those guys from the Youth of the Future campaign ads Gamal Mubarak sponsored. "The youth of our generation . . . how quickly we'll rise . . . hear! Hear!" Remember them? Anyway, the guy was a hottie, and he set my heart aflutter the second I saw him. I waited awhile at the microbus station for a bus to arrive. I got on, and he got on after me. I thought to myself: Why on earth would someone so chic-looking ride a microbus?! Something fishy was going on. Then he came and sat down next to me—oh my God! oh my God!—and I was worried he'd pull some moves, and I don't mess around when it comes to shutting those types down . . . Off with my shoes and bam upside their heads, Youth of the Future and Gamal Mubarak and anything else be damned! But halfway through the ride, he leaned over and said, soberly:

"Do you mind if I ask you something, ma'am?"

You don't know what happens to me when someone calls me "ma'am." I get weak in the knees. But I'm not easy or anything! So I put on my best stern face and said:

"Ask me something? What for?!"

"I just wanted to ask . . . are you involved? It's obvious that you're not married or engaged—you're not wearing a ring—but I have to ask to make sure you're not involved, ma'am."

"Ma'am" again! Oh my God!

"It's hardly appropriate to talk about things like this on public transport, you know. I don't even know you! And I'm not used to talking to people I don't know!"

"But what if I liked you, ma'am, and wanted to make a formal proposal? What am I supposed to do? Because, to be honest, I've been following you for a while, but I've only just worked up the nerve to talk to you."

Oooooh! Sweet! Following me for a while! He was totally smitten, then! But still, who did he think he was dealing with?! I had to play this right.

"Well, if you've been following me for as long as you say you have, then you've got to know where I live, and you've got to know who my father is, and he's the only one you can talk to about things like this. Please don't embarrass me anymore."

So put together! So very put together!

"You've just proven to me that I was right to choose you."

Ohhh yeah. That's the stuff! So far so good. I was acing it! I'd put him in his place, true, but I'd also said he should talk to my dad, so I'd left the door open.

Right then the ticket collector kid got snippy with me:

"Your fare, lady. Or are ya going to ride for free?!"

You little twerp, I'm trying to create a mystique here! Why do you have to go and humiliate me?! I reached into my purse just as our friend jumped in to pay for me.

"No, it's not right."

He said: "No, please. Let me. I can't let the woman I plan on proposing to pay when I'm around!"

And, GOAAAAAAAAALLL!! That was it . . . he was going to propose! Just like that! So, yes, I didn't know what he did for a living, or where he lived, or if he did celebrity impersonations, or what he was all about, but his getup said it all, really.

As soon as the microbus stopped, he got off with me, looked over, and said:

"I wanted to save you on the microbus. It's totally obvious you don't have any money."

I flipped out. Are you going to condescend to me, buddy?!

"It's obvious that your wallet's empty. End of the month and all. So there you go. Saved you a bus fare. It should help."

I looked at him, stunned:

"Where are you getting this nonsense from?! I've never walked around with anything less than 300 pounds in my purse!"

He said, mockingly:

"Naaaah. Don't believe it!"

At that point, my brain was about ready to explode. So I took all the money out of my wallet and showed it to him.

"Here, look: 50 . . . 100 . . . 200 . . . 220."

He reached over and took the money . . . looked it over, counted it, and said:

"So it's true. You do have money, all right."

And, in a second, he'd folded the bills and put them in his pocket:

"I'll keep these as a souvenir 'til I come round to your house to make that proposal."

I couldn't understand what was happening, and before I got a chance to say anything, he jumped on behind someone on a motorcycle that, come to think of it, had probably been following our microbus the whole way. And before you knew it, he'd pulled a Houdini.

So yours truly stood there in the middle of the street like a giant IDIOT. Like someone who'd been drenched with a bucket of mucky water. I didn't know whether to scream or to run after the bike or to hit myself. I stood there for a full five minutes, confused about where to go. Cars honked at me, and when the people inside them saw me looking so dazed, they probably thought I was deaf. Or crazy. Or one of those women who sells tissue packets on the street. People walking by stared at me. Little kids pulled at their parents' clothes. "Baba, Baba, what's wrong with that lady?!"

After a while, I turned around and walked into the hospital where I work with a detached expression on my face. I walked into the pharmacy, I sat on my desk, and I burst into tears. My coworkers huddled around me. "What's wrong?! What happened?! Did someone upset you? Did something happen?"

In the middle of all the crying and all the heaving, I could only blurt out:

"I got mugged!!!"

AAAAHHHHHH!!

# On Delicacy and Femininity

Remember that movie, *The Olive Branch*? The one with Ahmed Mazhar and Soad Hosny? No, not *El-Nasser Salah Deen*; that one didn't have Soad Hosny in it!

In the movie, Ahmed Mazhar plays Soad Hosny's teacher who falls in love with her and marries her but suspects there's something going on between her and Omar El-Hariri, another teacher at the same school. What does this have to do with anything? I'll tell you. Be patient.

In one of the scenes in the movie, Omar El-Hariri walks into a coffee shop where a bunch of his coworkers are sitting, and they ask, "What's the name of that nice cologne you're wearing?"

He says, "Femininity," and, aside from how stupid the name is—it really is a completely ridiculous name for a man's cologne—that was the first time I had heard the word in my life.

*Femininity.*

The word was associated in my mind with Omar El-Hariri's face for a long time, right up until I grew up and found it being used to describe people other than our friend Omar E.: Hind Rostom, Marilyn Monroe, and Laila Eloui, to name a few.* I began looking around at the people in my life to see if there was anyone the word could be applied to and, to be honest, I couldn't find anyone!

People, where is this femininity they talk about?! Mama spends all day in the kitchen, cooking. Tante Suheir, our neighbor, does laundry day and night and hangs it up on the clothesline, where

---

*Egyptian actresses. Hind Rostom was known as the Marilyn Monroe of the Middle East during the height of her career in the mid-twentieth century, and Laila Eloui, active since the 1970s, is also considered a great beauty of her generation.

it drips down on Tante Amal's balcony, so Tante Amal fights with Tante Suheir about the dripping laundry, and fights with her son because he's playing on the street and neglecting his math homework.

Or forget that generation. On to the next: Manal, my cousin who's five or six years older than me. Four years ago, God blessed her and she got hitched. Well, Manal, you've always been a pretty, girlie thing—show us what femininity looks like once you're married. A few months after she got married—bam!—she got pregnant. Swelled up and expanded in all directions, but never mind, she'd give birth and pull herself together soon after, right? But then Manal, our go-to example for all things feminine and all things laid back, started looking like one of those women in the butter and detergent commercials. Up all night because the kid's crying and up all day because the kid's father wants something to eat and drink. And her salary, which she used to blow on perfume and makeup, now goes toward three things: Pampers, Pampers, and Pampers. Of course, being up for twenty-four hours has started to take its toll on her face. And as soon as her head leans against any wall, anywhere, you can hear her snores even in outer space.

Or let's drop that ideal. Let's turn our attention to another equally strange notion about the Egyptian woman instead: the concept of delicacy.

A delicate girl looks shyly at the floor whenever you talk to her, makes you feel that she's so easily hurt the wind could bruise her, that she's a waif who'll snap in half if she does any walking. A guy gets engaged to a delicate girl and walks around making up poetry about her, calling her a breeze to deal with, a positive breath of fresh air. Her voice is the sound of birds chirping, and anytime a man listens to a sweet song he'll think of her . . . and change his ringtone.

When the breeze passes through your hair, my love,
   I hear it. It speaks of longing!
And the soft perfumes that melt into your skin,
   every time they touch you, they speak of longing!*

A man will invite her out to lunch and she'll only eat a salad. He'll buy her an expensive gift and she'll get upset and say: "Why did you put yourself through the trouble?!" And life will go on like a beautiful dream until the man is jolted awake. When?

A month after the wedding—or a week, depending on his luck—when the demands start and the changes begin, and when he realizes, all of a sudden, that everything has done a 180.

Because any woman with traits like these had to have lived in a bubble, completely isolated from other people. Never ridden public transport, never been harassed and forced to deal with an inappropriate guy and put him in his place. Never dealt with people at work, never been forced to take a stand and fight because someone violated one of her rights or because something unfair was happening to her. Never been to the market to buy vegetables, and certainly never cooked them. So, naturally, if she starts doing all this stuff after she's married, there's no way for her to keep being the delicate waif girl who's bruised by the blowing wind. There's no other option for her if she wants to survive married life.

Of course all of this gets worse and worse the second kids arrive on the scene and when the responsibility of raising them falls almost completely on her shoulders, and her shoulders alone. So her choice is either to toughen up and scare the kids and their father, or to risk having the kids raised badly and then having everyone blame her, and her alone.

So, beloved husbands everywhere, don't be upset when your brides turn into somebody else after you marry them. They don't

*Lyrics from a song by Egyptian singer-songwriter Mohamed Mounir.

have any other option. Maybe if you put in SOME effort and helped them, they'd have a little more time to look after themselves.

And, beloved husbands, when you're looking for partners, pay attention to their upbringing and their manners and their faith instead of focusing on things like "delicacy" and "femininity." Because qualities as rare as these change with time.

As for men who need femininity to last a lifetime . . . well, they can just look for bottles of cologne like Omar El-Hariri's.

# The Third

Rest in peace, Anwar. You are so missed.

Anyway, what was she saying? Who's the "she"? Oh, right, right, I forgot to tell you. My mother's friend "Auntie-Body" (her real name is Shukreyya but she's such a busybody that that's what her best friends fo-evah have taken to calling her) had found a groom for me.

"This groom, Bride, lemme tell ya, he's a MAN!"

"Well of course he's a man, what else am I supposed to marry? A motorcycle?!"

"No, I mean he's got this VIBE about him and this PRESTIGE and he's smart and he's levelheaded and he understands EVERYTHING."

"A suitor who understands things?! I doubt it. Honestly, I've yet to meet the type. But I guess it's possible. Fine, Auntie-Bo . . . err, I mean, Tante Shukreyya. When's this one coming over, and who's he coming with? Is he bringing his mother along?"

"His mother?! He he he. Sweethaaht, I told you, he's a MAN."

"Yeah, but, did his father self-reproduce to bring him into existence?! He has to have a mother."

"No, Bride, you've gotta understand, he's totally independent, and he has his own ideas, and he doesn't listen to just anyone, and he depends on himself completely."

Ooh . . . nice! Independent. Has his own opinions. Doesn't listen to just anyone. I go nuts for the type: Ahmed Abdel Aziz in *Money and Children*, Sherif Mounir in *Helmeyya Nights*, Muhammed Riyadh in anything he did before he married the Monster.*

*Egyptian actors known for playing independent, strong-willed characters. "The Monster" is a reference to Rania Mahmoud Yassin, an Egyptian actress and Riyadh's wife.

To be honest with you, I got goose bumps. I go *nuts* for the type! How great would it be if it turns out that he has teeth that crowd each other like Nabil El-Halafawy? Or ears that stick up straight like Hamdi Qandil? Or a double chin like Amr Moussa?* Men who have character, men who seem important, have to have little quirks like these. It's what sets them apart. Not to mention that good-looking people have scarred me for life. I want an ugly man. No more sleek politician types for me!

The fateful day arrived. We cleeeaaaaned the apartment and we beat the rugs and we washed the curtains that had just been washed two days earlier, and I ironed and put on my outfit and I slapped on some so-so makeup—all about quantity not quality here. If he turned out to be the type who didn't like a lot of makeup and got that cringy look on his face, I could go wash it all off and walk back out like God intended (he asked for it!). And if it turned out that he was the type who was into Technicolor, I had a strawberry-flavored lipstick I could go in and positively devour. So there! No one can blame me. I'm a full-option bride.

So we sat and waited, and then heard footsteps on the stairs, and—wham!—the doorbell rang in a way that just *screamed* levelheaded. Ohhh yeaaah! Great men will be great, after all.

He walked in the door and, oh baby!, he was about eight feet tall and broad. You know all those quirks Nabil and Hamdi and Amr have? It's like the doors of Heaven were wide open when I was asking for them. My, what ears he had! And what teeth! And what a sweet, sweet double chin that looked like it could be used for extra storage! He was wearing a pinstriped suit and a chic tie and glasses. It was like the minister of transportation himself was in my house, people!

We were all still standing at the door, looking at each other. I was ecstatic. The man had this all-important vibe that could

*Egyptian actor, media personality, and secretary general of the Arab League and former foreign minister of Egypt, respectively.

make you speechless. He could make a woman standing next
to him feel like nothing. There are a lot of girls out there who'll
tell you that they need to "assert" themselves in a relationship,
but here's a saying for you: the more you ignore a girl, the more
she'll steal your money . . . No, wait, wait, that's not the one I was
looking for. Sooorrry! I *meant* to say: the more you ignore a girl,
the more she'll fall for you. Yes, yes, that's the one!

We were still standing at the door when the guy peered out
at us from inside and said, "Come in, everyone! Why are you
standing outside?! Make yourselves comfortable."

We moved inside like we'd been hypnotized, and Baba looked
at me as if he were asking: Who is this person you've brought in
to boss us around in our own home?! And I looked back at him
like I was pleading: But I loooove him, Baba!!! AAAAHHH!!

He walked in, sat down, and crossed his legs. We were still
standing. He looked at us and smiled this classy little smile and
nodded his head as if to say: Sit down . . . sit down.

We sat down in front of him, enraptured, and we looked
at him the same way our doorman 'Am Muhammed's wife
looks at the pair of gold bracelets the dry cleaner 'Am Mostafa's
wife wears.* He was sitting on the chair across from mine. He
looked at me, then at the vase that was on the table. All of a
sudden, with no explanation, he picked the flower vase up off
the table, put it on the nearby armoire, and sat down again.
Baba looked at me and I could see the lines that resemble four
1s showing up bright and clear on his forehead. (A note: Baba's
angry forehead lines look like four 1s, not three 1s like regular
people.) The groom looked at Baba and smiled the same classy
little smile.

"It's just that I couldn't see her very well."

---

*'Am translates literally to "uncle" but is used, in a general context, to show respect to
an older man.

"Her," of course, being me. And it didn't take a genius to figure out that he could see my face over the vase and that what he actually wanted to see were my . . . oh God. Obviously Baba reached a similar conclusion because his eyebrows got so close to each other they were about to merge into one long line above his nose, which had gotten red, and his mouth, which was pursed because he was grinding his teeth. Mama reached over and patted Baba's hand, as if to say: Just wait, so we can see where this is going . . .

Baba gave her a look that meant: It's obvious that he's a sleazeball and needs to have his eyes gouged out!

She raised her eyebrows and sighed, which was meant to answer: All men are like that now. This is the generation of satellite television, my friend!

All of this went on as yours truly sat there, drowning in sweat, and all the while he was completely zoomed in on?! I don't know . . . And I don't want to know!

Suddenly, as abruptly as before, he started talking:

"Excuse me, can I comment on something?"

(And he pointed.)

Baba shifted enthusiastically in his seat, ready to perform his honorable fatherly duty and attack him, and I could see Mama slip out of her shoes in case she needed to use them in support of my father.

"Comment on what?"

"Your nails."

"Huh?"

"Your nails."

"What about them?"

And off he went like there was no stopping him:

"Why do you have them filed round? Don't you know square is in? Hey, what's in as far as gold these days, yellow or white? . . . The white paint you've used in this room is excellent, so is the color you've used in the rest of the apartment. Hey, do you own or rent? Renting is so expensive nowadays, by the way . . . The weather's cold these days. It looks like winter's coming early this year. Hey, you know, it's a leap year this year?! I was born on the 29th of February, so I only celebrate my birthday every four years, hahaha! One time, a guy tried to sit down at a café; he sat in tea instead, hahaha! I take my tea weak, with one sugar, Tante."

Mama, after being thoroughly assured of his insanity, put on her wooden face:

"We've run out of tea, dear."

"Run out of tea? That's okay; then I'll have coffee! Hey, doesn't the coffee shop downstairs bother you? Because being disturbed by other people's noise is the worst thing in the world . . . especially when it comes to people who talk too much.

"That's really a lot of makeup that you're wearing there, Miss . . . Miss . . . You haven't actually told me your name? Names are always important. So, are the officers in the police station next to you any good? Do they stop thieves from hanging around here? Because people are about ready to eat each other alive, I tell you . . . What are you eating for dinner today? I smell *mulukhiyah* and rabbit.* Rabbits† are really easy to make these days, by the way. You can invest a hundred pounds in the stock market and walk away with a rabbit . . . a million, that is. I've told Tante Shukreyya a million times that I want to get married. I don't know why it took her so long to bring me here!"

Baba stopped him:

"*I* know why . . . Get out!"

"Beg your pardon, Uncle? You mean get a job out of the country? No, I don't really intend to. See, I . . ."

---

*\*Mulukhiyah*, made from mallow leaves, is a staple of the Egyptian diet. Ladled over rice or eaten with bread, it is frequently served alongside rabbit.
†Colloquial Egyptian-Arabic for "millions."

"Out! Get out! There are no girls who want to get married here!"

"Hahaha, are you kidding around, Uncle?! Then who's this here?! Hey, will someone tell me what her name is? Am I going to marry someone whose name I don't know?"

"I said get OUT! We don't have any girls who want to get married here!"

"I don't understand . . . Are you being serious, sir? Are you kidding? This has got to be a prank! Oh, speaking of which, have you guys seen that hidden camera show Prank.com?"

And here, dear readers, my father's blood pressure reached heights never before seen among humankind. And he, at 5'6" and sixty-two years old, grabbed the 8'-tall groom, dragged him to the door, and pushed him down the stairs, where we heard him roll down in a way that just *screamed* levelheaded.

. . . Thank you very much for your condolences.

# Yes. Love . . . No. Love

Something's been bothering me lately . . .

A suitor? No, not a suitor. I'm taking some time off from the whole suitors business. You saw how that last one almost brought the world crashing down on my head . . . I've decided to take a little vacation so that you don't come across a headline one day about how I've thrown myself off the Cairo Tower or anything.

First off, everyone, you have to realize that the population of pharmacists is unlike the rest of the world's peace-loving peoples.

There was no official endorsement of the "Sweethearts System" in my graduating class, as was the case everywhere else. That's because, in our department, boys would shove, elbow, and trick girls out of the way so that they could beat them into lecture halls and grab the best seats. Naturally, there wasn't any room for romance. And in the labs, where a girl could get distracted for a second only to find that her chair had been swiped and her stuff had been thrown all over the floor because one of Egypt's conscientious men had gone ahead and decided to implement gender equality? I don't think there was much chance of a great love story developing there either.

So, given the circumstances, there were exactly six Sweetheart couples that we considered newsworthy in our class, the class before us, and the class after us. Now as far as our clique was concerned—and I was, in all honesty, its moral compass—Male-Free was the only way to go. All because of the advice beloved Mama had given me and which I'd imposed on everyone around me with all the harshness in the world.

"Ola . . . what were you doing over there?!"

"Oh, nothing . . . Sameh was just asking for my lecture notes."

"Whaaaaat?! Have you lost your mind?!"

". . . Why? What's wrong?!"

"Don't you know what's inside a lecture notebook?!"

". . . Notes on the lecture. What else would be in there?!"

"Paper, missy, paper!"

"What's wrong with paper?!"

"Paper is a means of communication! . . . First, he'll leave a letter in there for you, then he'll write you a poem, and before you know it, he'll be like, 'Will you marry me *'urfi*-style?!'"

"Oh my God . . . I wasn't thinking!"

"Well there you have it, missy! Now go get your notebook back this very instant!"

Ola ran and snatched the notebook from the guy's hands as he was standing with his friends, and said:

"Gimme that! You think I'm stupid or something?! I'm not that type of girl, buddy!"

Naturally, the schmuck's rep could've been dragged through the mud once people found out that he'd been putting the moves on a girl. Or, even worse, half the girls on campus could've launched an official boycott against him. I looked at Ola in victory.

"That's more like it! Who does he think we are?! This clique will forever be Male-Free! No nasty business here!"

One time, Abeer was sitting next to me in microbiology lab, and Omar Mamdouh—the only boy in our class who looked like he could've been a halfway decent human being—was on her other side. I spotted him turning to her and asking:

"Are we supposed to heat the sample first or stain it?"

I saw her about to open her mouth to answer his question and, all of a sudden, I was glaring at her. She looked at me, terrified, and looked at Omar, confused. She tried to open her mouth again, and I glared some more. She tried and I glared, she tried and I glared. Until she burst into tears, threw the sample on the bench, and ran out of the lab.

Ohhhh yeaaaaah! Now THAT is what it's like to strike the fear of God into someone, all right! Felt so guilty for thinking about talking to him, she burst into tears. Bravo, Abeer . . . Bravo.

Omar turned to me and asked:

"Uh, why is she crying?"

I looked at him and then turned the other way. Did he actually think I was going to talk to him?! . . . What was the world coming to?!

Now as far as I was concerned, I didn't need anyone to monitor my behavior. I was perfectly equipped to stop short anyone audacious enough to think they could talk to me.

"Excuse me, Doctor?"

"Yes?"

"Can I say something?"

"Is it about pharmaceutical chemistry?"

"No."

"Organic chemistry?"

"No."

"Biochemistry?"

"No."

"Toxicology?"

"No."

"Then, I'm sorry, we have nothing to say to each other."

And I would raise my head in pride as I left the guy standing there, his jaw hanging open like 'Am 'Abdo the doorman when he watches the Korean soap.

So we followed the Male-Free system the five years we were in school, and lived in total serenity and security and were completely at peace with our Being. Only the news of a Sweetheart engagement could ruin our calm.

Hearing the news would send Fatima, a clique member, to the verge of a nervous breakdown. She'd get a case of the nail nibbles, develop some serious third-degree finger gnawing, and nothing would put an end to it or calm her down except the news that the engagement had fallen apart. That Bibo had dumped Jiji, or that Jiji had blown off Bibo, or that Jiji's dad had blown both of them off after finding out that they'd been fooling around behind his back for five years.

Throughout all of this, and especially whenever I'd see one of those Arabic movies where three girls and three guys sit around loving on each other all day and get married at the end, I'd always say to myself: Nonsense! No manners there at all! What kind of upbringing have these people had?!

And anytime I'd catch a movie or a TV show where college guys would trick girls into marrying them *'urfi*-style only to dump them later, I'd tell myself: That's more like it! There's no messing around with morals! And I'd become even firmer in my principles.

Then we graduated and the tragedy that is living-room meetings began. A groom would walk in . . . and a groom would walk out . . . or sometimes it would be nothing but walkouts. And so began the torture that still hounds my life to this very minute.

One time, Tante Fadia and I were venting to each other:

"If you had found someone in college, wouldn't things have been a lot easier?"

"What?!"

I jumped out of my chair like I'd been electrocuted:

"What do you mean?!"

"I mean, there are a lot of girls out there who marry men they meet in college. They fall in love with each other and all . . ."

"Fall in love with who?! With each other?! How is that possible?! That is completely indecent! How am I supposed to know what a guy's intentions are?!"

"It's pretty obvious, sweetie. If his intentions are honorable, he comes to meet your family. Wouldn't that have made life a lot easier?"

Unn-unn-UUNNNNNN.

You know those silly scenes in black-and-white movies where twenty-five years after the main character has lost his memory, he slips on a banana peel and hits his head on a pole, and his memory comes back and his life passes in front of his eyes like a screen with a bunch of circles that get bigger and bigger? That's what I felt like then.

I stood there, staring at her. I couldn't understand anything at all.

So all that talk that our parents filled our heads with was wrong?! . . . Were all the Soad Hosny and Hassan Youssef movies right?!*

Is our society two-faced? Or is that just how you're supposed to raise kids?

Was I right or was I too straitlaced, or what?!

---

*A famous on-screen couple; their movies are popular even among families who disapprove of dating.

# The Fourth

Break your exam seals and get your pencils ready because I'm about to ask you an important question:

What are five things that Tante Shukreyya and Al-Qaeda have in common?

Eh? Give up? Here's what I've been able to come up with:

One: The two—regardless of whether we agree with them or disagree with them (you could, by the way, agree with Al-Qaeda, but it is impossible to agree with Tante Shukreyya)—will always be responsible for explosions and destruction and, more often than not, blood will be spilled.

Two: The two may disappear for a month . . . two months . . . three months . . . a year, even, and then resurface with a bomb even bigger than the one before it.

Three: Sometimes it seems like a conspiracy theory is the only probable explanation for their existence. Just as Al-Qaeda can seem like an American invention, Tante Shukreyya can seem like she does what she does because she might have had a thing for my dad a long time ago and now's her chance to get back at him and raise his blood pressure.

Four and five: You guys think of something because I can't be bothered.

So I was sitting on top of Moqattam* and Karim was in front of me, sobbing. His eyes were as red as tomatoes from all the crying:

"I beg you, Bride, we have to get married! I can't live without you!"

"I don't know what to tell you, Karim . . . The matter's out of my control."

*A hill in Cairo; Moqattam has both residential and recreational areas.

"But I don't understand. Why does your father hate me?!"

"What am I supposed to do, Karim?! I've tried, I swear, I've tried to convince him a ton of times and it's no use."

"Just please let me meet him, and I'm sure I can convince him!"

"How are you going to convince him, Karim?! You know there's no convincing Baba."

"But how is it my fault that he saw me hugging Mona when she was wearing that red shirt?!"

"You think Baba's the only one who saw you?! All of Egypt saw you!"

"Well, what am I supposed to do?!"

"There's only one solution."

"What is it?!"

"Don't star with her in your next movie."

Suddenly, the mountain started shaking.

"Bride . . . Bride . . ."

"Yes, Karim! I'm here! I'm here!"

"Karim who?! . . . Oh, God damn that Karim Abdel Aziz who's made you lose your mind!"*

"Eh . . . who's shaking the mountain?!"

"What mountain, missy? I'm your mother! Get up! Get up, girl, Tante Shukreyya is here and wants to talk to you."

The shock woke me up.

"Oh God, I leave Moqattam and Karim for Auntie-Body?!"

"Shut up, girl, don't be rude! Get up and get dressed and splash some water on your face, and come out and meet her."

"*Rise and shine, the early bird gets the worm* . . . Fine, I'm coming."

I walked in and found Auntie-Body settled comfortably in our humble living room.

"Taaannnte, how ARE you?!"

---

*Part of the new generation of Egyptian actors, Abdel Aziz is popular with young women.

"Hello, my little darling! Let's cut to the chase, Bride . . . I have found SUCH a good groom for you!"

"I know, I know. A man with his own opinions with a father who self-reproduced and brought him into existence all by himself."

"Hehehehe, oh you! . . . You know there's no joking around about this stuff! This groom's goooohgeous—no one's as good-looking as he is!"

"Listen up, Tante. You know I haven't liked the good-looking ones since that politician type came around."

"SSSSSSHHH! You'll get us in trouble! What politician type?! Are you still asleep or something?!" (My mom, while grinding her teeth.)

"Oh . . . right, right . . . I'm still a bit groggy. So tell me, Tante, how old is this groom?"

"Thirty-two."

"Good, and where does he live?"

"In Dubai, dahling, the land of *shobbing*! Hehe."

"And where does he plan to settle down?"

"Also there."

"Okay. And what does he do exactly?"

"He was a coach, sweetie, but he was such a genius they asked him to teach engineering instead!"

"Whaaaat?! How is that even possible?! Mama, how long was I asleep? Did the way the world works change in an hour?!"

"Honey, I'm just telling you what he told me! When you guys talk, you can ask him anything you want. He's coming by tomorrow at seven. You know, I feel reaaaally optimistic this time, Bride! You know I love you just as much as my Sausan!"

"Oh, hey, speaking of whom, why don't you ever bring any of these men you find to meet your daughter?!"

"Oh . . . er . . . I'll see you tomorrow at seven, Bride! Wait for me!"

Didn't I tell you this was all a conspiracy?!

Tante left and I started singing, my mom on backup:

"I feeeel a disaaaster coming oooon."

"Sweet Lord, sweet Lord!"

The fateful day arrived. The hands of the clock moved slowly toward the hour, completely unlike my own rapid heartbeats: da-dum, da-dum, da-dum, da-dum, da-dum, da-dum, da-dum.

Heartbeats that shook my core and quaked my being: for the time had come! My time with happiness, the time fate had delayed! But I was patient, and patient I was, and now it was time to reap what my patience and my waiting had sown! And here I was, taking the first steps toward my new kingdom, where there is no sadness and no tears! For I have drunk much from the cup of misery, and now all that remains is the cup of bliss from which I will be satiated for life!

CUUUUUUUUUUUUUUUUUUUUUUUUUUUTTT!!

You didn't actually believe that, did you?!

So, it was seven o'clock on the fateful day, and we sat there, waiting, after the round of housecleaning you all know so well. How long did we wait? It was seven o'clock . . . then seven thirty . . . eight . . . eight thirty . . . nine . . . nine twenty.

Baba was on his last nerve, grinding his teeth, his favorite hobby for those times when we get one of *those* grooms (I swear, I feel bad for the man's teeth. It's all my fault). Anyway, he was staring at me and huffing, and I was dying of embarrassment. Mama took him out of the room and I heard them arguing in whispers (So that they wouldn't "hurt my feelings." As if). I thought: Son of a you-know-what, you're doing this to ME?! By my father's teeth, if we end up together I'll take all this out on you and every damn person in your life! . . . God willing.

Finally, fiiiinaaally, at twenty-one hundred hours and forty-four minutes the doorbell rang. I was worried Baba would get his revenge by making bachelor and co. stand at the door for a while—an eye for an eye and all—but Mama looked at him and looked at me and then gave him a pouty stare. She must have gotten his fatherly instincts going, because he gave in . . . and sighed . . . and got up to open the door. They trailed in: Tante Shukreyya in an urban-trash couture dress, followed by the groom, who was basically thirty-two teeth that had sprouted a man.

Teeth—as in choppers. Yep. I swear. Widest smile I'd seen in my entire life.

I really liked his smile, personally, but of course it completely riled up Baba. He was late AND he was smiling about it too?! The "1111" lines started showing up on his forehead. But Mama put her right hand on his left arm, and he sighed again and acquiesced to the situation at hand (how much do you LOVE the word "acquiesce"?!).

We all sat in the family room, and talked about everything, everything that is but marriage. Like it was just a casual get-together, and nothing more.

The groom was handsome . . . yep, handsome all right . . . and he answered all our questions with a broad smile or a ringing laugh. Through his wide-open mouth, you could see his tonsils and his glottis and, if you *really* paid attention, you could spy his large intestines. But he was nice and cheerful and all, and he had a happy face . . . It would be fine.

Anyway, the visit came to an end, and what do you know?! He was the first groom who hadn't walked in completely empty-handed and walked out with Baba's hands ready to wring his neck! He'd brought a little wrapped package and, from the beginning of the meeting, I had been dying to find out what was in it.

As soon as he and Tante Shukreyya left, me and Baba and Mama gathered around the package. We formed a circle around it and no one wanted to reach out and touch it, as if we were FBI agents who suspected there was something in someone's bag in Tora Bora. Curiosity was about to kill me,

so I reached over and unwrapped the little package, and . . .
What was in it, you say?
??????????????????????????????????????????????????????
Patience, patience! I'll tell you at the end.
Baba looked at me and asked:
"What is this?!"
"I don't know, Baba. It is what it is."
Mama said to him:
"Well, you know, we don't really know what grooms are
supposed to bring on occasions like these . . . maybe this is
the fashion?"

Baba stood there, looking at us for a bit then looking at the
package, and then he sighed in resignation and shrugged.
". . . Maybe."

So the second visit . . . Oh, you'll be asking: Why didn't you
talk marriage details during the first visit so you could get it
over with?

People, it just isn't reasonable to have every guy who comes
to visit leave and never come back again! People are starting to
talk, and they're saying that if the men are leaving after the first
visit, then there has to be something wrong with Bride.

So we'd said we'd split all future meetings in two. This way,
if things don't work out, maybe people will think we just didn't
agree on terms or that we were the ones who turned the men
down and had Baba shove them down the stairs.

Stupid? It IS stupid, but what are we supposed to do? There's a
saying that goes: if you're in a country where they worship a calf,
then cut some grass as an offering. (It's not a very classy proverb,
I know. I heard it from Tante Shukreyya.)

So this first get-together was supposed to be an encouraging
thing and, aside from how late he was, it didn't have too
many drawbacks.

Now about the second meeting . . . We didn't start waiting around at seven like the first time, because we'd caught onto the fact that the groom seemed to be operating on Dubai time. So we started waiting at nine. See?! We're *totally* flexible people here!

The doorbell rang and the two walked in. Same routine as the last time around except this time Tante Shukreyya's dress was ghetto-vomit couture. I kept looking at the groom's hands to see if he'd brought anything with him, but my desires went amiss (what does "amiss" even mean?!). Anyway, Mr. Smiley Groom sat down . . . precious lil' thing!

Baba started things off with a wide smile: "How are you, son?"

The groom: "Hehehehehe, I'm good, thanks."

Mama, also with a wide smile: "You didn't have to trouble yourself and bring anything with you last time!"

The groom: "Hehehehehe, it was nothing, Tante. Just a little something from where we come from."

Mama: "Where you come from? Does Dubai have nice things like that?"

The groom: "Hehehehehe, Dubai? What Dubai, Tante? You mean Riyadh."

Mama: "Riyadh?"

We all turned to Tante Shukreyya, who looked a bit embarrassed, then flashed this nervous little smile and said:

"It looks like my hearing isn't what it used to be . . . Hehehe— age, you know."

We turned back to him and he was still smiling away.

Baba: "So you're in Riyadh?"

The groom: "Hehehe, yes. I live and work there."

Baba: "And how are you getting along there? Are you happy?"

The groom: "Hehehehe, very, very."

Baba: "And you get along with the Saudis there?"

The groom: "Hehehehehe, Saudis? What Saudis, Uncle? I don't know any Saudis."

Baba: "How do you live in Saudi Arabia and not know any Saudis?"

The groom: "Hehehehehehe, Saudi Arabia? What Saudi Arabia, Uncle?"

(This is where Tante Shukreyya grabbed her bag and tried to leave.)

Tante Shukreyya: "I'll just get out of your way since you've taken to each other so well. Let me know how it goes!"

This time, it was Mama who stood up to her:

"Wait a minute, Shukreyya—sit down! Where do you think you're going?! You wait right here until we figure out what the story is!

"What were you saying there, sweetie? You live in Riyadh but don't know anything about Saudi Arabia?!"

The groom: "Hehehehe, yeah, Tante. I mean, how would I know anything about it?"

Mama: "How is this possible, you imbecile . . . Riyadh is in Saudi Arabia!"

The groom: "Hehehehehehehehe. I get it! You guys think I'm from the Riyadh that's in Saudi Arabia?!"

All of us, in unison: "Then what?!"

The groom: "No, you guys, I'm from Riyaaaadh. The Riyadh that's in Domyat!"

Mama: "The Riyadh that's in Domyat?! I don't understand any of this!"

The groom: "Heheheh—"

Mama: "I swear to God, if you finish that laugh, it'll be the last laugh you laugh in your entire life! Now explain to me what it is you're talking about!"

The groom: "Okay, okay. No more laughing. Riyadh's a village in the Domyat province, Tante."

Mama: "Excuuuuse me?! Then where did this Dubai talk and *shobbing* talk and I don't know what else talk come from?!"

Baba intervened: "Okay, fine, fine . . . Now explain this to me before I set you and this idiot who brought you here on fire: What does your highness do for a living, exactly?! Are you a teaching assistant in the sports department or the engineering department?"

The groom got up and was half in the room, half out. Baba grabbed his arm and Mama grabbed Auntie-Body's neck.

The groom: "To be honest, Uncle, to be totally, totally honest . . . I *was* a teaching assistant in the sports department but then I kept needing assistance, and needing assistance, and then I failed, so they kicked me out and I transferred to vocational school."

Mama and Baba were holding the pair and inching closer to them the way vampires creep up toward their victims. They dragged them out the apartment door, and the groom's and Tante Shukreyya's faces showed pure, unadulterated terror. And suddenly, I stuck my leg out and tripped them, and the three of us watched as they rolled down the stairs together in glorious surrealist fashion. We dusted our hands off, closed the door, and turned off the light.

So, of course, you'll want to know what was in the package the groom brought with him the first time?

A round disc of honey treats, half a kilo of semolina pudding . . . and three pieces of baklava!

# In Defense of the Egyptian Woman . . . the Bully

On every street and in every corner and every traditional coffee house and every café and every crack-house, even . . . on minibuses and in taxis and on buses or even in rickshaws, Egypt's loyal men will have the same general complaints about their wives: "She's depressing . . . she talks too much . . . she nags too much . . . she growls all day and beats the kids up . . . she's made trouble with the neighbors . . . she has me completely broke and she's clipped my wings . . . she has the worst damn scowl." And, on certain occasions, you may come across one of them massaging his back or neck and gather that he'd slept to the rhythm of a beating from his wife's rose-topped slippers.

The problem is a purely Egyptian one, too. You'll try and tell me that men all over the world complain about their wives, and I'll say soooorry: the percentage of men around the world who complain about their wives is 20–30 percent . . . say 50 percent, even . . . but if you conduct a survey, Egypt will be the only country where the percentage of complainers is 99.9999 percent (as in everything else).

So I'm sure some people will think I'm here to deny all the accusations but, no. Not at all. No sirree. I will readily admit that I am an example of the bullying Egyptian woman. Yeah, that's right. I'm a bully, even though I still haven't gotten married. I may not have any male property on which to implement the women's bully code, but I can't fight the impulse inside of me. We're talking about genes here, people. The whole thing about Egyptian women being bullies didn't just start today or yesterday, either. This thing has its roots way down deep in the dredges of history. You'll find, for example, drawings on ancient Egyptian temples that show women holding whips. They'll pull a fast one on you and tell you they're holding the "keys of life" and stuff, but don't you believe it . . . those were just the instruments used back in the day. The ancient stand-in for rose-topped slippers and the mortar. You want more proof? Don't all depictions of ancient Egyptian men show them with their heads covered and none of them is ever bareheaded? Aaand why is that? Because if a guy back then had gone bareheaded, he would've exposed the bumps and bruises on his head and his standing as a man would've been in doubt among the other Pharaohans!

So why is the Egyptian woman a bully? Yeees! THAT is the question I've been waiting for. The Egyptian woman, in all honesty, can't be anything *but* a bully. I see a bunch of people shaking their heads, not liking where this is going . . . Well, honestly, what is the poor thing supposed to do?! A man proposes and she says yes so she can have a wall of support to lean against, only to find, as time goes by, that she has to be that wall, and the ceiling and the floor to boot!

She wakes up in the morning and makes breakfast and gets the kids dressed and feeds them and feeds her husband, and sets off running. She drops off the kids old enough to go to school at school and the ones too young for school at her mother's, and she runs off again so she isn't late for work, but then gets there late anyway and is written up. After she gets off work, she goes to pick up half the kids from school and the other half from her mother's, and drops by the market to get some vegetables, and goes home dragging the kids behind her—or being dragged behind her kids—and helps the kids change, and starts cooking. After she's done cooking, she sets the table, and after she sets the table, she washes the dishes and makes the tea and sees if there's any laundry or cleaning to be done. After she's done with that, she helps one kid out with homework and fights with another one because he's hit his sister and yells at a third because he's ignored all his drawing paper and is coloring on the walls instead. And after all this is finished, Mr. Special, whose sole responsibility in life is to go to work and come home to eat and sleep, trudges in from the coffee house and looks at the woman who's been busting her butt all day and says:

"What kind of getup is that to greet your husband in?! Why don't you stop scowling for a change and go put something nice on, since you've just been sitting around all day. It's not like you have anything to do!"

And then he's surprised when she busts his head open with the mortar!!!!

Oh, and the problem isn't just that an Egyptian husband will ignore his wife, there's also his complete lack of shame: Anywhere that involves standing in line, like the train station, for instance, a husband will "innocently" suggest that his wife stand in the women's line because it's shorter. So she'll get in there and shove and get shoved, and after she finally gets the tickets, she'll get yelled at. "What took so long?!" And sometimes, when a woman will get into a fight on a bus, her husband will jump in and say, "Let ME deal with this!" and Mr. Macho will put on a big show of pretending to hold her back when all he really wants to do is hide behind her. What'll really grate on your nerves, though, is when a husband thinks that having full access to his wife's salary is a God-given, Qur'an-sanctioned right. So you'll find him, his pseudo-pious face on, saying:

"I don't *need* your salary; it's just that I saw Sheikh So-and-So on TV and he was saying that women who don't hand over their salaries to their husbands at the beginning of every month are cursed in this lifetime and the next, and I'm really just worried about your soul, honey . . ."

And seconds after she hands over the money, he does a 180.
"Can you help the kids out with their homework?" she'll ask.
"I don't feel like it."
"The gas cylinder's empty. We need a new one."
"And how is that my problem?"
"Well, can you at least put that cup you just used in the sink?"
"Then what are you here for?"

And then he's *so* surprised when she rips him apart with her bare teeth while he's sleeping!!!

Another important issue: the whole scouring for money thing. A man will always accuse the Missus of waiting until he falls asleep so that she can go through his pockets and grab any money she finds. That's aside from the bits she supposedly takes out of the grocery money and the money she hides under the loose tile. Oh reaaaaaallly?! Well, *he* takes all her money and gives her an allowance that's so tiny it'll enrage you, and *he* gives her a twenty and says he wants *mulukhiyah* and rabbit for dinner, and every two or three months *he'll* say: "I'm in a tight spot, Umm Hamada.* Why don't you see if you have any money you can loan me?" And when it's winter and the cold nips at the kids, and she tells him: "We need to buy a heater." *He* says: "How?! We're living day to day here." And when she gets some money out from under the tile to buy the heater herself, then *she's* the sneak who's been stealing from him.

And then he's surprised when she chops him up into pieces and packs him into garbage bags!!!

You're so upset? Then leave her, buddy! What's forcing you to stay?!

But the good ol' Egyptian man is all talk. He isn't like the Indian man who'll fight with his wife and then pour kerosene all over her . . . and he isn't like the American who'll off his wife

*Umm means "mother of."

with a bullet to the head, throw her in the nearest river, and then pretend to look for her missing body with the police . . . and he isn't like the Frenchman who'll suggest that his wife find a boy toy to calm her nerves a little. The Egyptian man is all talk, talk and nothing else. Naturally, I'm not saying you should be setting fire to us, but if you feel so trapped?! Then leave! If you can't leave, then gather up all the chairs and put an end to the giant pity party you've thrown yourself.

Men of our beloved Egypt: be ye gentle with thy maidens . . . so that the maidens don't bring your entire world crashing down on your noggin and give you more reason to complain.

# The Fifth

"Ayman's here! Ayman's here!"

That's the beginning-of-the-day signal in our office—
something like the "Long Live the Arab Republic of Egypt!"
that started our school assemblies when we were kids. After
someone yells it out, it's like a desert storm blowing through our
office: hand mirrors are brought out, lipsticks of all different
shades and colors, eyeliner pencils; head-scarves are loosened
and retied; hair is patted and put in place. All the primping that
a little princess does before she meets her Prince Charming goes
down at that very moment.

All of this for Ayman. Ayman who? Ayman is the only
employee of the male sex in our office. Imagine, for a second,
fourteen women pharmacists of prime marriageable age (although
the prime age thing is questionable for some) and . . . Ayman.
And not just any Ayman. Broad-shouldered, strong-jawed, wide-
smiling, piercing-eyed, Roman-nosed . . . basically, the owner of
all those characteristics Nabil Farouk has given Adham Sabri and
has been driving us crazy with for twenty years . . . Ayman.* So
he's definitely worthy of all the primping.

"Thereheis." (That's me . . . sighing.)

Anyway, after the desert storm, Ayman walked in. Nobody
could look directly at him because of the blinding light. The
hair, the smile, the leather jacket, the shiny shoes. You couldn't
take it all in in one go. You couldn't open your eyes with the
smell of his cologne drifting everywhere. It made two women
speechless and made a third lose consciousness, and it was

*The protagonist of Farouk's literary series *The Man of the Impossible*, Sabri is described
as an attractive, highly skilled member of the Egyptian intelligence.

making a fourth willing to lose a whole lot more than her
consciousness if she was only given the chance.

"Morning, everyone."

"Gofhtbeityuison." (That's us, stammering out gibberish
and giggling.)

Ayman stood there for a bit, looking around the office, and
then his eyes landed on me. Then he smiled at me. And I basked
in the glow of that smile until I was rendered temporarily blind
by its brightness. And then . . . and then . . . oh my God, and
then he walked my way. Where was I supposed to go?! What was
I supposed to do?! I pretended to be busy with some papers in
front of me, but he wasn't buying the act and was still headed my
way—and everyone was staring—and suddenly my body was
drowning in its own sweat. The amount of sweat that I perspired
in that moment could've solved the drought problem in Ethiopia.
And I don't even want to tell you about my face. My face was so
red that if you'd painted a 22 on it, people would've thought it
was Abou Treika's soccer jersey.[*]

He leaned over my desk and, in a quiet voice, said:

"Good morning!"

"Huh? Wha? Uhhhh. Okay."

"Can I talk to you for a bit?"

"To me?! Swear! I-I-I mean, er, why?! Is there a problem?!"

"No, everything will be just fine, God willing."

I tried to get him to spill the beans and asked:

"What do you want to talk to me about?"

"Something good . . . something that relates to the future."

(A white wedding dress and trills of joy and a ring . . . Saad
El-Soghayar[†] singing at my wedding and Nawal the belly dancer
dancing.) . . . All of that ran through my head in that very

---

[*]Second striker and attacking midfielder for El-Ahly. One of the most popular soccer
players in the team's history. Abou means "father of."
[†]Egyptian folksinger popular with the working class.

instant. Nawal who?! Nawal is a super important belly dancer!
You guys just don't know her because you're ignorant.

"When?"

"Can we talk after work today? Is that okay?"

"Of course we can talk after work!" (I raised my voice when
I said this to rub it in.)

Now the rest of the day . . . it was the stuff of legends! Like I was
living in an Arabic melodrama. I spent all day with my head down,
while the other girls formed alliances against me and acted catty.

The two on my right: "Who does she think she is, exactly?!
All this because he wants to talk to her?! Well, so what?!"

The two on my left: "Pretty soon she'll start thinking she's
Nancy Agram and then no one will be able to even talk to her."

Two others, as they were dispensing medication to patients:
"If he knew what she was *really* like, he wouldn't look at her
twice. Just ask me. Here are your drops, sir. When your
condition acts up, put a few drops of this in your nose."

And so the day continued. Catty talk, and more catty
talk . . . and that was in addition to the glares. I mean, if looks
could kill, I'd be in the central morgue right now. The one person
who stuck by me through all this was my friend Noha. She kept
me strong and helped me keep it together. Smiled at me all day,
and patted my arm. Bless you, Noha! Now that's what friends are
for! Every now and then, Ayman looked over and smiled like he
was saying, Never mind them, and every time we accidentally
made eye contact, I looked away (I'm shy, all right?!). But Noha
wouldn't let any of it get to me. Bless your heart, Noha!

Then business hours were over, and for the first time in the
history of the Ministry of Health, people didn't want to leave.
The clock struck two . . . two ten . . . two fifteen . . . and no one
wanted to budge.

Noha tried to salvage the situation:

"Hey, people . . . you not going home today, or what?!"

One of them: "I still have work to do."

Another: "Yeah, and Baba might drop by to pick me up."

A third: "I don't feel like going home yet. Whoever wants to buzz off, er, I mean, go home, can go home."

Ayman sneaked a look at me and was clearly completely embarrassed. And I was about ready to die (You sons of . . . why so desperate?! You're going to find out everything anyway! Do you have to cramp my style?!).

I waited until it was two twenty-five, and still no one wanted to move. So I figured I had nothing to lose.

I grabbed my purse and got up, and I can't explain where all the courage came from, but I walked up to Ayman:

"Dr. Ayman?"

He jumped:

"Yes?!"

"I'd like to speak to you, please."

And I walked out of the office quickly, and he followed, relieved that he'd gotten an out. I heard a commotion in the office: everyone was trying to get up to follow us as quickly as possible so that they could watch. They probably caused a mini-stampede, given the size of some of them . . .

I went to the hospital cafeteria and, with all the confidence in the world, sat down at the nearest table. I couldn't believe any of this was happening. (This was the *rendezvous* cafeteria!! Thank you, God. Thank you for making all my dreams come true. I can now die happy.) Ayman sat down across from me, all shy and looking at the floor (I thought: No, please, listen, now's *really* not the time for shyness. There's a herd of girls on their way over here, and if they arrive before you start talking, I'm going to get up and butcher them all or throw myself out the window like they did at that massacre at the Muhammed Ali Clay Citadel).*

---

*A play on the name of a citadel built by Muhammed Ali Pasha, widely considered to be the father of modern Egypt. In order to eliminate his greatest political competition, Muhammed Ali invited Mamluk leaders to a celebration at the citadel, only to trap them inside and kill them.

"Yes, Dr. Ayman? Talk, talk. Don't be shy!"

"To be honest, it's kind of a sensitive issue." (Yes! He was talking. God, I love sensitive issues.)

"All good, I hope?"

"I'm sure you know I've been working here for seven years, ma'am. That's aside from my job at a pharmacy outside the hospital. So, I'm pretty comfortable, financially speaking."

(Yeeeeees! This is what I'd wanted to hear all along. Who cares about "I love yous" and "I'm into yous"?! As long as he starts off with "I'm pretty comfortable, financially speaking," then things might actually work out.)

"That's great for you, Doctor, but what does this really have to do with me?"

"To be honest . . . uhh . . . I . . . I mean . . . I've been thinking of settling down."

(Wheeeeee!!! Justice will prevail! Justice will prevail!)

"Oh, seriously?! You haven't settled down yet? I had no idea!"

"No, I still haven't. And the thought's been growing in my head since I started working here."

(Oh yeah! Oh yeah! That's what I'm talking about. Now get started on the important stuff.)

"And what does this have to do with *me*?"

"What does this have to do with you?! You're the person this has to do with the most!"

(The world's spinning, people. Someone hold me still, please.)

"How so?"

"To be honest, I'm hoping you'll . . ."

"Yes?!"

"Well, that you'll . . ."

"Yeees?!"

"Talk to Noha for me."

"Noha?! . . . Noha who?!"

"Noha who works with us in the office. I've noticed that you're the person closest to her, so I thought you'd be the best person to talk to about this."

(Axes and gunshots. A noose like the one your ol' uncle Saddam went down in around this idiot's neck, and next to him, that Noha chick. And I'm holding the lever and, bam, their necks break.)

"Noha?! You've brought me here so you can talk to me about NOHA?!"

"Uhh, actually, it's you who brought *me* here, not the other way around."

"Excuse me?!"

"Yeah, I'm actually worried Noha will be upset about us talking like this."

"Do you have NO feelings?! Or do you just not understand anything at all?! Huh?!"

I got up and the cafeteria workers stared at me like they were watching a scene out of *King Kong*:

"Are you SO dumb you actually brought a woman here . . ."

"You brought me here . . ."

"*Shut up*! Just . . . just don't talk at all! You've brought me here to be your little love messenger?! Cat got your tongue so you can't talk to her yourself?!"

"Miss, I just wanted . . ."

"I said don't say anything!"

That's when I noticed that I'd grabbed onto the ashtray on the table and that he was cowering in his seat and looked scared of me and that the cafeteria workers were about to call security. Or maybe they were calling the morgue so they could come clean up after this was done.

I gathered that I wasn't looking super great right then, especially since the patients had started coming out of their rooms to watch. I let go of the ashtray, adjusted my clothes and my head scarf, and plastered a huge smile on my face:

"In any case, Dr. Ayman, you can talk to Noha in person. 'Sensitive issues' like these really shouldn't involve middlemen. Excuse me."

I turned and walked out of the cafeteria, and the guy just sat there, stunned. I remembered something so I turned back. He saw me, and ran off to hide behind Umm Tarek, the cafeteria lady:

"Oh yeah, by the way, when you get married, don't forget to invite me to the wedding. Okay?! Bye now!"

So what happened after all this? . . . I'm not entirely sure.

Ayman, bless him, went off to Libya. And word is he's gotten married to someone from over there.

Noha . . . Noha is my giiirl! My BFF! What?! You think friendships fall apart that easy?!

# Habby Falantine

Happy Valentine's Day, everybody. Bit late, I know. How am I supposed to know when the thing is, anyway?! All I noticed was that there were teddy bears upon teddy bears when I was walking down the street. I say, hey, maybe it's Childhood Appreciation Day! I walked around and saw red clothes upon red clothes. I say, hey, is El-Ahly playing today?! Feel better soon, Abou Treika! I saw a ton of people walking around carrying red hearts. I say, those must be the blood donation people! Ages later, I was at work, minding my own business, when I found Mrs. Sundus (a pharmacist who works with us; she's married so we all call her Missus—she's the only one of us who's ever achieved the honor) talking to Noha (you'll remember her, of course).

"I walked into my apartment and the light was out and the man had lit a couple of candles and put them on the dining room table and, let me tell you, I lost it: 'Are you blind, you idiot?! How can you think it's okay to put candles on the tablecloth?! Do you not know how much that cost?! Isn't it enough that my daddy bought it himself?! Is it because you didn't have to pay for it? You think you've gotten me for cheap, don't you? If we'd made you pay everything you had for the furniture, this wouldn't be happening!' So the man stood there, and looked a bit stunned, and then he walked over and turned on the light. I looked over and I saw a bunch of red stuff on the table. Get this—he'd gotten me flowers! I looked at them

"Habby Falantine" is a tongue-in-cheek reference to the way many Egyptians pronounce the Valentine's Day greeting. Arabic contains no distinction between the letters *b* and *p*, nor between the letters *v* and *f*.

and I saw that there were ten of them. I said: 'You crazy man, aren't those the type of flowers that you make jam out of?! Tell me where you got them from so I can return them and get a kilo or two so we can stock up on some jam.' The man stared at me for a bit, then he packed his bags and went off to his mother's . . . Men . . . He has *no* idea how much effort it takes to make the jam so he can eat it all up in a second. What really gets to me is that I have *no* idea why he got so upset. Huh? You got any idea?"

Noha, who looked like she was having a stroke, stared at me:

"Can you say something, please, because I can't get any words out after that!"

I looked at her funny:

"Why are you so worked up?! The woman did nothing wrong. If he wanted some jam, he should've just asked, instead of putting her through that whole charade. She'll have to keep nagging the flower man to get the type you can make jam out of!"

"ARGGGGH (that's Noha screaming and hitting herself) . . . Woman, it's Valentine's Day today!!"

"Oh riiiiight! It IS today! No wonder everyone out there looks like they've been dunked in tomato sauce!"

Anyway, we finally understood why Mr. Shafei, Mrs. Sundus's husband, was acting so strange, and Sundus interjected to blame his mother for giving him a wishy-washy upbringing that made him pay attention to silly little things like that.

As far as I'm concerned, I'd be happy if anyone gave me anything, some arugula leaves, even. I could sit and brush my hair at night with the moonlight spilling over everything in the room (Isn't "spilling" a good word? Romantic, isn't it?), and I could think of my dreamboat and listen to one of Shafiqa's mushy, dreamy, romantic songs (Shafiqa, you're so amazing! Such a glorious bunch of romantic songs you have).* And I could sit and

*Egyptian working-class singer.

tear the arugula leaves off one by one. *He loves me . . . he loves me not . . . he loves me . . . he loves me not . . . what the?! Is that a worm?! Couldn't he have cleaned the leaves in some vinegar before he gave them to me?!*

And you know what, people? I feel like there isn't any old school romance left these days. It just doesn't work anymore. Take a look at the mushy black-and-white movies: the Shadia and Salah Zulfikar one where they run toward each other in slo-mo screaming, "AHMAAAAAAAAD . . . . MOOOOOOONAAAAAAAA." The entire plot of the movie is that he's leaving on a train; she tries to get on the train but misses it, so she leaves a message for him with the train official; the train official tries to catch him but doesn't, and so they don't end up getting married, and spend twenty years looking for each other. How are they supposed to make a movie like that now?!

In today's movies, as soon as the lovers separate, and because the woman's cheap, she'd give the man a missed call on his cell so he could call her. And because he's an even bigger cheapskate, he'd send her a "Call me, please" text so that she ends up paying for the phone call. So either the poor girl gives in and calls him or gets stubborn and thinks he's a good-for-nothing and a deadbeat, and proceeds to delete him from her cell phone and her life. And that would be a love story as brought to you by Naguib Sawiris.*

Or how about *The Postman*? The story is that Shukry Sarhan, the postman, reads the letters of a girl who falls for a guy and sleeps with him. And when one of her letters accidentally burns while Shukry's reading it, the lover never learns that her father's found out about the affair and wants to kill her.

If they had had access to email, the whole thing would've ended as soon as the guy found out that there *was* no girl and that one of his buddies had been messing with him.

---

*Egyptian businessman and founder of Mobinil, one of three cell phone service providers in Egypt.

Or, he would've gone to propose, and the whole thing would've fallen apart over who was supposed to pay for which piece of furniture. Where's the romance then, huh?!

Even this whole Falantine thing. It wouldn't be the same if people found out that they were actually celebrating the holy day when our brother, Saint Falantine, sat on top of a pointy stake and croaked. Yep, I swear—that's the story behind the celebration!

Plus, I think that people are just messing around these days. After work, I walked around gift stores to browse, and I saw these two girls who looked like they were from the countryside, trying to find a present:

"Hey, gir', should I gittim the heart or the teddy beah'?"

"No, gir', you stupih?! What beah'?! You givin' dis to a maaaan! You think men play wit' beahs?!"

"I just dunno, gir'. I dunno bout dis heart. It's so *small*."

"Gittim two, then."

"Whaa?! Two?! What fo'?! Not like I'mma marry 'im."

And there you have it. Falantine's Day and the type of people who celebrate it. Just call it a day, why don't you, and don't bother?!

# The Sixth

Do I miss the grooms? God save you . . . no. I don't miss the grooms at ALL. They've depressed me and every time I fall asleep, I have nightmares where their stories merge into each other: One time, I dreamed of Ayman holding up two pieces of baklava, and of the politician type riding a microbus on his way to Riyadh. Another time, I dreamed of the Amr Moussa look-alike and, in the dream, I was standing in front of him clutching an ashtray menacingly. Two or three other times, I dreamed of Karim Abdel Aziz. But that's a whoooole other story.

Another sign of depression that'll hit someone like me, someone who's been through a solid number of solidly crazy experiences, is that they'll get to the stage where they don't even want to hear the word "groom" anymore, not even the tiniest whiff of it (and if there's any kind of smell emanating from a groom, then no thanks . . . ). The doorbell will ring and I'll go hide behind Mama. The phone will ring and I'll grab Baba's hand before he can pick it up and look at him in panic:

"No, Baba, please. Please, no. Don't do it, Hagg!!"*

"Do what, sweetie?! What is going on with you?!"

"It might be Auntie-Body with another groom, Baba. I beg you, don't answer the phone . . . treat me like you'd treat your own flesh and blood!"

". . . My own flesh and blood?! Umm Bride, the girl's lost it!"

Mama came over and disentangled my hand, which had been grabbing onto Baba's like a crab claw.

---

*Term used for someone who has gone on pilgrimage to Mecca. Also used as a sign of respect for older people. Hagga is the feminine.

"It's all right, sweetie, it's all right. Your fate will turn out just fine, I promise. Just calm down now, sweetie. Praise the Prophet."

"Aaaaahhh, no, Mama, no! I don't want anymore Auntie-Body ever again!"

"It's over, sweetie, it's over. May she never come near you again."

Thank God the doors of heaven were wide open that day. Mama should've picked a better prayer like "May you get married tomorrow morning" instead of it being all about Auntie-Body, but still. Better than nothing.

So then what? So then God gave me a break from Auntie-Body, and sent me Uncle Disco as compensation. Uncle Disco (his real name is Disouky) has been Baba's friend for ages. He's all chic and good-looking and cool, and he looks like he leads the comfortable life that he does and . . . what?! Marry him?! What're you talking about?! I said he's my DAD's friend. You think I'm so desperate I don't have standards anymore?!

Anyway, Uncle Disco always comes over to our house to play a game with Baba. Checkers?! Where did that come from? Poker?! Pfsh, get out of here. How dare you?! No, they play PlayStation. Yeah, that's right . . . Uncle Disco is a heavyweight.

So every time, he sits there beating Baba . . . and beating Baba . . . until a fight breaks out and Baba throws the machine on the floor, and the brawl that ensues can be heard by the coma patients all the way over in the intensive care unit of Kasr El-Einy:

"You just don't know how to play!"

"You don't know *anything*!"

"Get outta here! You know as much about PlayStation as Shaaban Abdel Rahim knows about atomic energy!"*

Mama and I will then get in there to break it up. And I'll get caught in the crossfire of punches and shoves. Afterward, Uncle Disco will cling to Baba in a hug, and Baba will say:

*Illiterate Egyptian folksinger.

"The devil's a smart one, Hagg Disco!"*

And he'll say:

"Forgive me, Abou Bride!"

And the story repeats itself every Thursday, like clockwork. It's gotten to the point where the neighbor's kid will bring his friends over on Thursdays to watch the fight. Explosions, and high-speed chases on the balcony, and head-butts, and tumbling. Better than any of those Sakka movies they talk about.†

Last Thursday, Baba got the PlayStation and the chairs ready, and I finished the round of push-ups and weightlifting I do to prepare for breaking up the fight. The doorbell rang and I went to open the door, and Uncle Disco poked his head in and, in a tone that made me really, really uneasy, said:

"How you doooooing, Briiiiide?! How's it gooooing?!"

You know the tone I'm talking about here? The one where people stretch out their syllables before they tell you they've brought you a bar of chocolate, and then, after you've worked yourself up daydreaming about some Cadbury, they hand you one of those brown Coronas that you can get for twenty-five piastres? Yeeeeeep. I knew something fishy was up.

"Where's your daaaaaaad?!"

"He's not here . . . he's gone to Iraq . . . he's gotten a job there . . . bye now."

I was about to close the door when the clever thing stopped it with his leg, pushed it so far open I got plastered to the wall, and walked in.

"Hehehehe, what job, you lil' rascal?! Oh Bride, you've always been the funniest! Ever since you were a little thing and now that you've blossomed into a gorgeous bride!"

Aha! Everything cleared up the second he called me a bride. And that wasn't all. If my extensive life experience has taught

*In Islamic and popular thought, the devil is believed to cause strife between people.
†A reference to Egyptian actor and action star Ahmed El-Sakka.

me anything, it's that when the word "bride" occurs in the same context as the word "rascal," then something really bad is about to go down.

He walked to the balcony, which he knows all too well, and I was so stunned I flopped down onto the nearest chair and waited for fate to come crashing down on my head. A short time passed, and I could hear some laughing and chuckling, and then I heard Baba call Mama. Mama came out of the kitchen, where she's spent half her life, and walked toward the balcony. I dove at her feet:

"Please don't, Mama! For the love of God, please don't!"

"What is going on, sweetie?! What's the problem?!"

"Don't go out there, Mama! I have a bad feeling about this! I think it's a trap!"

"What're you talking about, a trap?!"

"I think Uncle Disco has brought me a groom."

"Well, so what, sweetie?! May God send more and more! . . . Weren't you so desperate to get married you were ready to claw your own eyes out?!"

"No, Mama. That's it. I'm done! I know what my luck is like now. Only imbeciles come meet me. I'm done, Mama! I'm going to live with you forever and listen to everything you say and do the dishes."

"Seriously? . . . You're seriously going to do the dishes?!"

"No, nuh-uh. Don't take advantage of this . . . Just please, for the love of God, please don't go out there!!"

"Don't worry, Bride. You know Uncle Disco's got his head on straight and is perfectly respectable and knows respectable people. If he's brought you a groom, then he must be respectable!"

I looked at her with tears in my eyes. She's clever, that mother of mine. The rascal. She was playing the same game she used to play with me a long time ago. "Go to school and I'll buy you some lipstick." . . . What?! I was in the third grade! A fully blossomed bride!*

Oh God. "Rascal" and "bride" together again. But Mama was right. Uncle Disco *is* a respectable guy and *totally* unlike Auntie-Body. If he'd brought me a groom, then he had to be respectable.

I got closer so I could eavesdrop. I stood at the door to the balcony, polishing the door handles with all the innocence in the world, and then I heard the fateful word . . . well, actually, three letters:

"Oom."

And that is, of course, the second half of that godforsaken word "groom."

Let me tell you . . . my knees got shaky and my heart began racing and the world started spinning and my face got yellow and my eyes got wide (God, Bride. Another imbecile this time, or what?!).

Mama came off the balcony and found me sitting Indian-style on the floor because my legs couldn't support me anymore. She dragged me up with one hand (strong, my mom is; built sturdy), and pulled me into a hug and gave me a kiss on both cheeks:

"Congratulations in advance, Bride!"

"Oh God, what's going on, Mama?"

"Uncle Disco has brought you a groom!"

And, suddenly, I dropped down out of Mama's sight. I collapsed onto the floor and sat Indian-style again.

"Daaaammmn it!"

"But why, Bri-Bri, sweetie?!"

And—bam!—she'd dragged me up off the floor again.

"This groom? He's respectable-respectable! The entire government's approved him already!"

*Popular way to refer to girls as they get older.

"The entire government?! Why?! Has God smiled down on a representative in the People's Assembly and sent him my way? . . . Wait, are you serious, Mama?! God, I would make *such* a good First Lady . . . in the future, I mean. I'd devote all my charitable work to children who've been victims of Egyptian television! . . . Or, no, you know what?! To minibus drivers who've been victims of seat belts! Or, no, no, you know what?! To women who've been victims of liposuction!"

"Whooaa there. Take it easy, take it easy! Where'd the People's Assembly come in?! What representative?! Your groom is *much* more important!"

"More important?! You don't mean . . . the presid . . ."

"SSSHHH, you're going to get us in trouble! Look, open your ears up wide and listen to me . . . What is the first thing that comes to your mind when I say police detective?"

"Squad cars, and a police station, and someone being violated with a broomstick."

"A broomstick?! I said he's a *detective*, not a janitor!"

"You're a sweet little thing, Mama. There really isn't much difference anymore. The same instruments are being used in both jobs now."

"Oh, stop driving me crazy! I'm telling you Uncle Disco has brought you a groom who can't be turned down. A police detective, and he's from a good family, and he's *very* well mannered."

"Oh yeah?!"

"I swear, Bride, it looks like it's actually going to work this time, sweetie!"

"Let's keep our fingers crossed on that one . . . When's he coming?"

"Next Monday."

"Alrighty then . . . We should start cleaning."

Of course, after the cleaning and the polishing were done, the house was spick-and-span all over. The fateful moment arrived:

the clock struck the hour, and the doorbell rang. Yeah, that's right . . . precise and organized. I'm a big fan of these on-time types. I've always secretly wanted to marry someone who's never late. Maybe because my own schedule is exactly like the trains'. Completely unreliable.

He walked in, and I stared and stared from behind the curtain that's about to fall apart from all the staring I've done behind it. Lean and athletic and tall and broad and deep and high and wide. He had this charisma going on that radiated from him, even from the back of his neck.

I thought: Oooh, Bride, oooh! *This* is more like it! I can be a detective's wife, and I can waltz through any checkpoint and say what I've always wanted to say: "You little piece of *scum*, don't you know who you're talking to?! I'm Detective So-and-So's wife! Don't you know who that is?!"

Ahhhh, yes. Power is sweet! It looked like Uncle Disco was a positive treasure chest, the sweet thing. I was standing behind the curtain daydreaming about checkpoints and prestige when I glanced up and saw the groom's eyes piercing right through the curtain that I was hiding behind. I thought: Yikes! What kind of eyes were those?! He probably just has to look at a suspect to get him to own up and confess. Well, that's good. He doesn't need any janitor's tools or plumber's tools or anything like that at all . . . Still a problem, though. How am I supposed to skim money off the household budget and hide it from him with those eyes, for God's sake?! If he just looked at me once, I'd give him everything I had. Not a problem. Not a problem. I could work it out; I could find a way.

Mama handed me the obligatory tray and I carried it in. He stood up right away. Well that's nice and polite! He had about three and a half inches left before his head hit the ceiling. But what's wrong with height?! It's mighty! So we settled in and the evaluation began. I pretended to be calm and looked at the floor, and every now and then, I peered at him out of the corner of my eye for a second or two. He really was much better looking from this angle than from behind that curtain. Not cute-cute, but still—he had manly features with a reasonable smidgen of handsomeness.

Now he, on the other hand, stared right at us. Anytime anyone spoke to him, he shifted to face the person talking and gave them this ridiculously penetrating look. Mama started talking, and he turned and looked at her, and she stopped mid-sentence and scurried out like she'd done something wrong. But Baba? Baba was *solid*. Didn't I tell you he was a PlayStation champ?! He just kept on talking and looked right back at the groom. And the groom looked right at him. And he looked right back . . . Bravo, Baba! You give him some of those looks that'll strike the fear of God in him! . . . But who were we kidding? Baba couldn't see the international staring match to the finish. A bit more staring, and he disconnected just like Mama. I felt sorry for him. But I was still super happy about our friend there. *Totally* solid . . . good stuff, I swear. *This* was the wall of support I'd been looking for since forever. Somebody you could lean against so you could walk into any kind of trouble with all the confidence in the world. Oh yeah! Now we were talking! This was the . . . And, at that very moment, his eyes landed on me. Ouch! I swear I could feel my face hurting. Where was I supposed to go!? What was I supposed to do?! I thought, Get up and make a run for it after your mother, but then I thought, No, stop it, girl, that's rude! Besides, I had to prove that I was a heavyweight myself. "I'm not the type who messes around . . . I've been strong my whole life." Shh, shh, who asked for song lyrics now?! Not the time!

He looked at me. And he keeeeept oooon looking at me. And for the first time since he'd sat down, he spoke:

"What's your name?"

"Bride."

"Full name?"

"Huh?"

"Full name! Don't you remember your own name?!"

"I remember! I remember! My naaaame . . . my naaaame? Huh? Uncle Disco . . . why don't *you* answer?"

Uncle Disco cracked up:

"You little rascal, don't you know your own name?! Her name, Mister, is—"

He raised his hand to stop him, and Uncle Disco gulped down the rest of the sentence.

"I asked *her*. So *she's* the one who should be answering."

Oh God. Why was I such a moron?! I couldn't say anything, and I was just about to open my mouth when he took something shiny out of his pocket. Ooooooh! Was it a ring, or a bracelet? Yes! He clearly had class. Classy people always bring gold gifts. He held it up with the tips of his fingers and handed it to me.

"What do you think?"

I reached out to grab it before he could change his mind and put it back in his pocket. As soon as I got a hold of it, I was surprised:

"What is this? A lighter?"

"Yeah. Nice? Do you like it?"

"But I don't smoke . . ."

"I know, I know. I'm just showing it to you. Do you like it? Take a look at it, Uncle."

Baba looked at it from a distance:

"Yeah, it's nice."

"No, hold it. See how heavy it is. It's twenty-four-carat gold."

Baba took it and rolled it around in his hands for a bit, and said:

"But I don't smoke either . . ."

"Good for you. Best decision you ever made. Can you call Tante in so she can see it?"

"It's all right, son. We believe it's gold, I swear."

"No, still, please call her in."

"It's all right, son. I said . . ."

*"Call. Her. In. Please!"*

He said that last line in a way that made the blood run cold in my veins. It's okay, Bride. You can teach him to be gentler in the way he speaks. We don't want to ruin this just as it's getting started. It's all right, Baba. He'll be your son-in-law soon enough, and then no one will be able to mess with you.

Mama came in after Baba called her, looking scared, and admired the lighter:

"Very nice. May you get more and more nice things."

He jumped up and grabbed it from her.

"No . . . it's mine! . . . I just wanted you to look at it."

Uncle Disco jumped in and asked:

"Can I see it?"

"No . . . you don't have to see it, Uncle."

And he handled the lighter with the tips of his fingers and put it in his pocket and walked toward the door.

"I'm going to take off, then. Good meeting you. I'll be in touch with Uncle Disco, and he can let you know about when we'll meet again. Excuse me."

And, whoosh, he turned around and walked out of the room and opened the apartment door and left. We were still standing there, and we had no idea what was going on.

Baba looked at Uncle Disco:

"Hagg Disco, what's going on here?!"

Uncle Disco, laughing:

"Hehehe, it's all good, Abou Bride! He's a powerful man, and he isn't into dillydallying. If he says he's going to be in touch with me, then don't worry. Congratulations in advance!"

And, whoosh, he turned around and left too.

Mama, poor thing, couldn't handle it anymore and threw herself into a chair, gasping:

"There is NO way I can give my blessing to this marriage. NO way. Good God . . . what was with all the terror?!"

"Oh, come on, Mama! What're you so scared of?! Have you done something criminal and now you're afraid you're going to get busted?"

"Get out of here, you big crazy! Are you actually defending him?! He could drag you to jail anytime you two got into a fight! Didn't you see the way he was looking at us?!"

"Mama, he's just . . . passionate!"

"Passionate?! If he marries you, he'll crack your head open! He reminds me of Ahmed Zaki in *The VIP's Wife*."*

Baba interjected:

"Umm Bride, we still have to see how this is going to end. Don't rock the boat, and let's just wait and see where this is going."

"That's the spirit, Baba! He's not a *huge* disaster. I can't chase away a groom every day! I want to just be done already!"

"Oh yeah?! Well, we'll just see where all your talk is going to take us!"

Obviously, I didn't get any sleep that night. I kept daydreaming about the detective and police checkpoints and the badges that were on his uniform, and about making everyone's life a living hell with his support. With all that thinking, I couldn't fall sleep until Fajr.† After I got up and prayed, I asked God to forgive me: "That's it, God, I'm done. I won't make anyone's life a living hell, and I won't run any red lights, and I'll be a law-abiding, model citizen." But, of course, after I didn't get any sleep, I couldn't go to work the next day, so I stayed home. The whole day, Mama was praying

*A popular Egyptian film in which Zaki plays a politician who emotionally and physically abuses his wife.
†Dawn prayer.

and sighing. Like she was trying to tell me: Let's just see where you're going to take us with all this.

And so the day passed. The next day, I went to work. The minute I walked through the hospital doors, 'Am Muhammed, the doorman who greets me with a prayer every day, turned his face the other way. (What was going on here?!) It looked like his wife had woken him up with a fight, or put him to sleep with a beating from some of those rose–topped slippers. Anyway, it's not like I was going to stand there and prod him and have him vent to me. So I just went on my way to the office. I met Mrs. 'Awatif on the stairs:

"Dr. Bride?"

"Yes, Mrs. 'Awatif? Is everything okay?"

"Yes. I would like to see you in my office for a minute."

"Now?"

"Please."

I walked with her to her office in Human Resources, and every time I passed by someone, they looked at me and shook their head.

What was going on, people?! Had everyone been put to sleep with a beating from some rose-topped slippers, or what?!

"Yes, Mrs. 'Awatif. What's going on?!"

"Mr. Hussein, Mr. Fotouh . . . some privacy please."

What was going on?! This looked serious. If I'd stolen something, they would've sent me to Legal . . . but Human Resources?!

"Tell me, Doctor, do you have any problems in your personal life?"

"What kind of problems?!"

"You know . . . Are you okay financially? Does your father provide for you well?"

"Mrs. 'Awatif, what is going on here?! Why are you asking me this?! You have my file. You know what my dad does for a living, don't you?"

"Well . . . okay, think of me as your mother. Be honest with me. Have any of your friends gone astray and dragged you along with them?"

"What?! Have you lost your mind, lady?!"

"Well then, why was there a detective from the vice squad here yesterday, walking around asking about you?"

"Vice squad?! Vice squad?! What vice squad, lady?! I don't know anyone who's had run-ins with the vice squad!"

"Then why was that man here, asking about you?!"

"A detective?! Vice squad?! . . . Damn him to hell!"

I couldn't take it anymore, and I couldn't think straight. My brain was paralyzed. I grabbed my purse and ran home.

"Help me, Mama, help me!!!! . . . Listen to this CATASTROPHE . . . I'm done for!!! I'm ruined!!!! I'm as destroyed as Zamalek in the soccer league, Mama! Aaaaaaaaaaaahhhhhh!!!!"*

Naturally, when Mama found out, she screamed her head off and called Baba and made him rush home, and when she told him what had happened, he went off to drag Uncle Disco over by the neck. And Uncle Disco, after a thorough tongue lashing from Baba, decided to hold a press conference, and called Mr. Future Interior Minister himself. The whole conversation took place as we were about ready to explode and as he sat there cooler than the biggest chunk of ice you've ever seen in your life.

"How could you do this, you moron?!"

"What did I do?"

"Did you send a detective from the vice squad to ask about my daughter at work?!"

"Well, naturally! Did you think I was going to go around asking about her myself? What's the point of officers, then?"

---

*Zamalek is notorious for its poor performance in recent national tournaments.

"You think you're investigating a criminal here?! She's a bride! And you couldn't find anyone to send but a vice squad detective to ask about her at work, either?!"

"Well, of course! Vice squad detectives have the most experience asking about girls and what they're up to. The one I sent to ask about *you* is from narcotics."

"Would you look at this?!!! You sent someone to ask about me too?! In a second, you'll be telling me you sent someone to ask about my wife!"

"Of course! He's from the embezzlement task force, though."

"Are you kidding me, you idiot?! You've shamed all of us!"

"Shame does not come to good people, Uncle."

"Look at you! All wise and eloquent! And so have all your investigations shown you that we're criminals, then?! When are you going to drag us off to jail?!"

"No, no, Uncle. The investigations have shown that you're all spotless, and your fingerprints have checked out too."

"Excuse me?! Fingerprints?! Did you pull our fingerprints up from the system to examine them too?!"

"Of course not, sir. You know that a new set of fingerprints has to be taken every three months. I did a new set for you."

"Oh did you now?! How'd you take us to get our fingerprints made without us knowing, then?! Did you drug us?!"

"No, Uncle, I have your prints."

We looked at each other.

"Our prints?!"

He answered like he was stating the most logical thing in the world:

"Yes. From the lighter."

"OH MY GOOOOOOOD!" (That's me screaming.)

There's no need to tell you the rest. All you need to know is that were it not for Uncle Disco's intervention, we would all be rotting in jail right now.

# Here and There... Now and Then

After what happened, I got a little case of the blues. Normal stuff, you know? I was asleep one night, and I woke up at three in the morning and I lay there, staring at the ceiling. That was when I realized I was twenty-eight years and seven months old. That is, that I'd gone past the twenty-eight mark and was moving, with solid footsteps and unshakeable determination, toward my twenty-ninth year of life. Someone will say: "And this hadn't occurred to you before?" and I'll say: "Nope. I swear." You get distracted by life, forget to pay attention, and all of a sudden, the truth hits you upside the head . . . A panic attack, some accelerated heartbeats, a tight chest, an EKG, and a couple of Inderal 40 mg later and it had passed. Completely normal. Happens to me every six months or so. You'll be tempted to think that I'm always kidding around, that I kick the world upside its butt, but who are we kidding? As the saying goes, moving cars have to crash . . . or was it sailing boats have to sink? In any case, something that's moving has to be destroyed!

In the midst of my depression, I stumbled across a notebook I used to write in ages ago, back when I was in college. Naturally, the "ages ago" factor didn't help, because it reminded me that I graduated seven years ago, and that I was a freshman twelve years ago, way back when Ruby was eleven years old, and Nancy was twelve, and Elissa was forty-five.* God. That's a whole lifetime ago . . . Ahhh, well!

I sat and flipped through the notebook. Part of it is a journal I used to keep, where I'd write silly things like:

*Ruby, who goes by her first name, is an Egyptian singer, and Nancy Agram and Elissa, who also goes by her first name, are Lebanese singers.

Today, when I was lighting the Bunsen burner
in chem. lab, I burned the edge of Ola's scarf.
Good thing she didn't notice until we were on the
microbus, and good thing she blamed the guy sitting
behind her on the bus who was smoking. Ha! Serves
him right. That'll teach him to never smoke again.

Another entry:

Today, as I was injecting a mouse with a solution
that was either salt water or cyanide, the needle went
through its body, came out the other side, and pricked
my finger. I wonder what the symptoms of cyanide
poisoning are . . . God, I hope it turns out okay.

Most of the entries were about cute little things like that. Another
part of the notebook had messages my friends had left me:

Here's to the crappy memories and the days of torture! . . .
If you start to forget me, remember to remember me! . . .
What has been will never be again! . . .

And more stupidity along those lines.

The third section was poetry. Yeah, that's right. I was a poet
back then. Well, not a poet-poet . . . but let's just say that if I'd
run into Shaaban Abdel Rahim, we could've made some really
sweet art together.

The first batch of poems was from my formal Arabic phase, and
the first poem I wrote is called "The Rain Drops Are Falling."
I wrote it during the middle of an organic chemistry test, after
the walls of the exam tent we were sitting in had torn, and after
rain had drenched my paper, ruined it, and forced the proctors

to get me a new copy of the test. Instead of doing what I did on the first test, which was leave everything blank, I wrote my magnificent piece of poetry, thereby fully earning my failing grade in organic chemistry. Although, it's obvious that Dr. Shams liked the poem, because he gave me a D instead of the D- I actually deserved.

So I became a huge celebrity in my class. My poems were such a hit a friend of mine asked if I'd write her one to give to a guy in our section. It seemed they had had their own little love story going on, but it had fallen apart. And you know me, I just LOVE helping out with things like that.

This girl, Ghada, was in my discussion section. She used to get chased around by a ton of guys until she'd gotten together with this one kid. A short time after they started seeing each other, Bibo blew Jiji off and gave her the mother of all silent treatments. The girl came running to me in the middle of a complete nervous breakdown and asked me to write a poem that would put the guy in his place, remind him of who he was dealing with. I got super, super touched by it all and wrote her the piece I consider to be the crown jewel of my entire collection:

> Know yet not, verily
> That I, whom they call Ghada
> Carry advice and wisdom aplenty?
> To all by lovers betrayed
> To all whose hearts were pained?
> And those who wished to weep
> And drink their coffee deep
> Upon my speech were cheered
> And restored to their lattes?
> Alas, despite my wisdom, I gained not a shilling
> And into a fisherman's net, I fell like a herring

And spent my nights spilling
My tears on a pillow.
Your love was like a goal
That eluded a goalie's catch
But now I am prepared
So take heed!—you've met your match
My heart, in your hands, will never be snared.
© Bride, 1998

Ohhh yeaaah! How glorious is that?! How can someone so
obviously dripping with poetic artistry like that let go of her talent
so easily?! . . . Anyway, my friend Ghada gave the poem to the guy
and—bam!—he transferred to Bani Sweif University the next day.
It's true that she'd let the air out of his tires three or four times,
and keyed his car two or three times, and called him 420 times
a day until he just couldn't take it anymore and ran off—but the
poem must've gotten to him, too! I mean, my words are bullets!

Now this second poem is from my vernacular phase. I swear,
I rolled around laughing after I re-read it the other day. I thought:
Good God, Bride, it's like you've *always* been thinking about
this . . . like you could sense what was going to happen to you.
It's like I was holding a crystal ball and looking into the future.
Here, look, check out what I'd written:

I don't want no white knight on a horse or an ass
I don't want Haitham's good looks or Abdel
    Gabar's class
I don't want no dreamer to love me day and night
I just want a nice guy, to share my insight

Check out Hatem. He came to visit with his mom
The day we went out, she had to come along
He got me a present; I said, "I love it!"

He said, "Well, that's great, cos my momma chose it!"
I took off running with all my might
I just want a nice guy, to share my insight

Saw Osama. I was scared of his arms
He had so many muscles, they set off my alarm
It can never happen! I thought and protested
On the night of our wedding, he'd probably get
    arrested
I didn't want a man who could kill me in a fight
I just want a nice guy, to share my insight

Amgad came around, I had to be sure
Didn't want to be swept away by his allure
He wrote me poetry and sang me songs
Made me feel like a princess. Is that so wrong?
But talk is cheap. I got bored of his tripe
I just want a nice guy, to share my insight.

© Bride, 1999

Now there's some transparency for you. I'm so transparent,
I could rival Nazif's cabinet.* Oh the memories!

---

*A reference to Ahmed Nazif, the prime minister of Egypt since 2004. In response to
accusations of hidden government corruption, Nazif and his cabinet frequently refer to
their policies as transparent and worthy of the public's trust.

# The Seventh

The worst part of my day, actually, ONE of the worst parts of my day (because it's such a heated competition, I can't decide which part is worse than the next) . . . in any case, the part that has a tiny lead on the rest of the bad ones: the walk from my apartment to the door of the building, and vice versa. Because on this back and forth, I run into nearly every single one of my dear neighbors. Generally speaking, neighbors can either make up a big part of your life or mean nothing to you at all. MY neighbors, on the other hand, are friendly. Caring. Concerned. Comforting. Completely unbearable people, in other words.

They love nothing better than to find out about every little thing in my life and butt into my business. Really, they help me achieve some balance in life (who turned on the self-help TV show?!) because no normal person should go around in a constant state of optimism and happiness (What?! Yeah, I'm an optimist . . . You got a problem?!). There has to be some depression mixed in, sprinkled with some infuriation to boot. Every cup has to have an empty half to balance out the full half. Or else the cup might spill on you and drench your clothes, and then people may think that you've wet . . . never mind . . . Back to our story.

The walk from my apartment to the door of the building is supposed to take a minute, but it can take up to a quarter of an hour some days. Each minute passes by slowly, and I always feel like there's something heavy weighing on my chest and that I can't breathe, just like when I'm about to watch Moataz El-Demerdash on TV or that Tamer Amin.* . . . The women will

*Television presenters known for their support of Mubarak's regime and the NDP.

always stop me as I'm walking by and shower me with hugs and lips pursed in sympathy.

"I hope things work out for you, daahhling!"

"Don't you be upset! Nice girls finish last."

"Are you still . . . ?!"

"Still?"

"No news?"

"Still?"

"Still?"

Naturally, you'll understand why the letters that I hate the most (and I can't even remember how many letters there are in the alphabet right now) are *s* and *t* and *i* and *l*.

The men always insist on stopping me too, and they praaaaay and pray for me. And I aaaameeen in response. And they praaaaay, and I aaaaameeen.

"May God bless you with a good husband!"

"Aaaaameeeen!"

"May God bring good news to you and your family!"

"Aaaaaameen!"

"May you find a couple of boxes of baby formula in your pharmacy for my kid!"

"Whooo's paaayiiing?!"

The worst days are when I run into Amani, who is three years younger than me, and who has Hind, who is now six years old. Yep, yep. She got married when she was nineteen. Back then, I was laughing hysterically and calling her an idiot. What could she possibly know about marriage or responsibility at that age?! How could she even figure out how to pick the right man?! . . . And the days passed and confirmed the wisdom of the saying: if it weren't for you, my tongue, my back would get no beatings. I heard Amani's mother say that once when I was walking past their apartment. She was trying to rub it in because I wouldn't get with Amani's brother-in-law and was yapping some nonsense about "choosing right" and "getting married at the right age" and a bunch of garbage like that. Anyway, the days, the months, and the years passed and proved, irrefutability, that all the opinions I had about marriage might as well be classified as science fiction. Just look at Amani, who has Hind (and another one expected to make an appearance any minute now that she's planning to call Mo'men).

So that things are even clearer, you guys have to understand that Amani and her husband, Mr. FouFou—I think his name's Abdel Fattah or something—are two peas in a pod. If compatibility were measured on a 10-point scale, they'd score a 12.5. The only problem they have to deal with is their fights over money. Money for groceries, money for the girl's school, money for makeup (his and hers). And it's pretty clear that, as far as their personalities go, she's like the twenty-five-piastre coin with the hole in the middle: all shiny on the outside and empty on the inside. And he's like the ten-piastre note: around but completely useless, and totally ignored by everyone.

One day I was tiptoeing down the stairs so that nobody would hear me walk by and—wham!—their apartment door opened, and I thought to myself: Girl, just jump onto the railing and ski your way down. But, no, no, no. I'm a respected pharmacist and if someone sees me, what exactly am I supposed to do then?! Anyway, what I was afraid would happen happened, and I saw Amani drag Hind out, her belly sticking out in front of her with Mo'men in it. It was obvious that he sleeping in there with one of his legs crossed over the other, because the shape of her tummy was borderline creepy.

"Get moving, girl, you're driving me crazy! I don't know who drives me crazy more, you or your brother . . . Oh, hey! Bride . . . how are you, sweetie?!"

"Hi, Amani . . . how's it going?"

"The girl's driving me up the wall, and the boy's stuck inside of me and won't come out . . . Hey, speaking of being stuck . . . no news?!"

I chose to ignore the jab. I didn't have time to get into a thing with her:

"Let's hope it all works out! . . . Excuse me."

"Wait, wait! . . . You know, if you hadn't gotten all conceited and if you'd just gotten with FouFou's brother, wouldn't your life have turned out just like mine?!"

"It's all fate, Amani. What can we do?"

"Yeah, I suppose you're right. Second time's the charm! FouFou was just talking to me about this one guy . . . EXACTLY your type!"

"I doubt it."

"Woman, will you be optimistic about this already?! This guy . . . he's polite, and he's religious, and he never misses a prayer! FouFou didn't like him at first because of something that happened a long time ago, but I pressured him into setting this thing up."

I looked at her belly:

"You pressured him?! And he's still alive?!"

"Hehehehe. Oh, Bride, you're funny, you crazy thing! Does next Thursday work for you? Good. I'll bring him and his family over. And you put something nice on, and don't wear any makeup . . . Remember, I said he's religious."

"Yeah, well, if you and Mr. FouFou are going to be bringing him over, you two better pay attention to the makeup thing, too."

"Huh? Yeah, yeah, okay. But, listen, you gotta work it, sweetie, okay? We don't want any more people laughing at you."

"Any more what?"

"Never you mind . . . hehehe . . . people are just cruel."

"Speaking of cruel people . . . how's your mother?"

"Huh? Oh, good, good. She says hello."

"Hello right back at her. May she be rewarded according to her intentions . . ."

"Amen. And may God have the best in store for you. Hey, tell you what . . . carry my girl down the stairs, will ya?"

(Aha! And so begins the tit-for-tat.)

"Fiiiine, Amani. Don't forget to give my best to Mr. FouFou, and tell his brother I hope he's not still upset."

"LouLou?! LouLou's a doll! He's a total sweetheart and he never holds grudges. If you'd married him, you would be living in total bliss right now!"

"Oh, hey, what did he end up doing about those bounced checks?"

"Oh, that'll work itself out."

"And the public drunkenness charge?"

"It'll be fine."

"And the sexual harassment suit?"

"God'll help him."

"And the *khul'* case his wife's filed?"*

"May he come out of it victorious! You know, if they get that divorce, there's still a chance you two could get together. Maybe God has destined you for each other."

"You think?"

"Yeah, it's totally possible! Why not?!"

Excellent question! Generally speaking, my extensive life experience has taught me not to judge grooms based on the matchmakers. I mean, I've met some complete bums through perfectly nice people—Auntie-Body and Uncle Disco, among others. I thought: Don't diss this, girl. What've you got to lose, Bride? Maybe this new groom she was talking about would The One, after all?

---

*Divorce proceedings initiated by the wife.

"When our land is thiiiiiirstyyyy, we water it with our
blooooood, something, something, something hard wooooooork,
our land's blessing grooooooows."*

I found myself, on the fateful day, singing that perfectly
romantic ditty to myself. It's incredibly romantic and touching,
but I was upset because I couldn't remember all the words, and
that made me feel like the day was jinxed. I racked my brain,
trying to find another romantic ditty, something by the beloved,
the magical, the ever-classy Shafiqa, but my memory failed me.
Anyway, in the end, the song that settled into my gray cerebral
cell matter was this delicate little number:

"A minute of mooourning . . . a minute of mooourning . . .
a minute of mooourning."†

The smooth beat relaxed me, and I started getting ready
for the fateful day. I pulled all my clothes out from the
closet and started looking for something to wear. I'm not a
hypocrite . . . There's NO WAY I'd change my lifestyle for
anyone . . . that would be cheating! Duplicity! Hypocrisy!
Lies! Buuuut . . . it wouldn't hurt any if we stood on some
neutral ground. I pulled out a red outfit. Tsk, tsk, tsk, red?!
God forbid! No, no, no. Besides, he might turn out to be
a Zamalek fan like Mr. Precious, since Zamalek types are
popping up all over the country these days. Hmm, how
about the fuchsia outfit? . . . No, no, what am I talking about,
fuchsia?! The name of the color alone is enough to have him
dole out a fatwa! Well, let's go with the yellow . . . No, no, no!
Yellow is a skanky color . . . never mind. And I kept pulling
out color after color, and outfit after outfit, and I wasn't
comfortable with any of them.

*Lyrics from the 1969 Egyptian film *The Land*, which chronicles the oppression of
peasants by landowners. It is notoriously depressing and extremely unromantic.
†Lyrics from a song by Tarek El-Sheikh, an Egyptian singer popular among the
working classes.

Finally . . . I found this white puffy thing on the door of the closet. Ahhh. It was either my grandma's mosquito net or the parachute my uncle used in the October War . . . Who says there weren't any parachutes in the October War?! You think you know more than my uncle?! He personally confirmed that he jumped down into Sinai with a parachute on October 6, 1974. And if he says it's true, then I believe him. I mean, why would he mess with me?!*

I had my little moment of pride, thinking of my uncle and his acts of heroism, one of which inspired the creation of a video game my dad and Uncle Disco play each week. I decided that, with a bunch of pins and a little bit of hemming, this would be the perfect outfit for me to wear to make my entrance in front of the groom, all in white from head to toe . . . a neutral ground color. Besides, there was a big chance this would work because the parachute, my uncle had told me, was lucky, and there was no way anything bad could happen to anyone who wore it: like that one time he was parachuting down and four Israelis opened fire and he danced around the bullets and danced around the bullets, and landed, safe and sound, on the roof of their house.

I reached my hand out for my makeup kit and then snatched it back quicker than I snatch my salary out of Mr. Rizk's hand at the beginning of every month. I decided to follow Amani's advice and not wear any makeup. This was an incredibly difficult decision for someone like me who never leaves her room without the daily fixin's. Like I said, there's NO WAY I'd change my lifestyle . . . buuuut, one day without makeup would give my skin a bit of a rest, at least.

I left my room to get started on the cleaning song and dance routine that we do every time, and I found Baba sitting in the middle of the living room floor, with a cup of tea and the paper.

*The October War was the 1973 Egyptian-Israeli war over Sinai. Her mention of the war being in 1974 is a deliberate mistake.

"Good morning."

"Morning."

"Anything new in the paper?"

"Well, naturally . . . Are you waiting for someone?"

"No, not really."

"Then where are you going?"

"I'm going to clean with Mama."

"What's this? Is your mother here too?"

"Well, where else would she be?"

"And you plan to stick around for a while?"

"Baba . . . what's going on?! This isn't the onset of Alzheimer's, is it?"

"Baba? Who's baba?"

He walked up to me and peered closely at my face:

"Who are you?"

"Baba . . . it's Bride . . . don't you recognize me?!"

"Bride? . . . Bride? . . . Ahhhh, yes, Bride! What have you done to yourself?! Do you have makeup on or something? You look really strange."

"Oh. Yeah . . . I'm just trying out a new brand."

Thank God the groom had never seen me before. And hopefully Amani and FouFou would keep their mouths shut.

After the rounds of cleaning and after I had adjusted the heroic parachute to fit me while maintaining its basic shape and looseness, the doorbell rang. Baba opened the door and saw a couple of people he didn't know.

After some resistance and denial and attempts at persuasion, Baba finally accepted that the people at the door were Amani and FouFou. He shook his head and said:

"I don't know why people look so different! I need to get my glasses changed."

I walked into the living room with the usual tray of gâteaux, and I looked around at the people who were seated.* Were those two over there Amani and FouFou?! . . . Probably, yes . . . I recognized them from their clothes. They were surprised at what I was wearing, but not as surprised as I was at the way they looked. Especially FouFou. Would you look at that?! He *could* look like a man after all! He even had the beginnings of a moustache that was striving really hard to prove itself! Too bad it was the right moustache in the wrong place. In between Amani and FouFou, I spied little Hind moving her eyes from her mom to her dad with an expression that looked like one a penguin would have if it fell asleep at the North Pole and woke up to find itself in Banha.† Poor thing. She was probably in the middle of a nervous breakdown and must've thought she'd been kidnapped. I felt bad for the crazy little thing. But it wasn't the time to feel bad, Bri-Bri! We had to focus on what was important. I bent my head and looked at the floor . . . the move I'd spent three hours practicing. I'd never bent my head down in front of anyone. Firstly, because I'd never been arrested, and secondly, because I like to look into the eyes of the person in front of me when I'm talking to them. I wouldn't change my lifestyle . . . buuuut, I'd always wanted to pay closer attention to the color of our rug. What d'ya know?! It really is a very nice rug, people! It had some blue in it, and some red, and some . . . BS 48. No, that wasn't part of a zip code written on our carpet. That was what the groom was wearing on his feet: brown sandals, size 48. Arrrrrrgggghhh. I got an off-putting in my being, located in the depth of my emotions. Sandals, Bride?! It's come to this?! You're going to marry a man who wears SANDALS?! But no, I wasn't going to be fussy. At that point, I was ready to marry any

*Gâteaux, which often comes in a box containing several different types of mini-cakes, is traditionally served by hosts at social gatherings.
†Banha is a city in northeastern Egypt; it is markedly less cosmopolitan than Cairo.

multi-celled organism that was alive, as long as it was willing to
snatch me out of the storefront that is singledom. The sandals were
*not* a problem. I thought: You can get him to change them. So, yes,
it's true that people say you can tell a man by his shoes. But that's
all backward thinking, and there was no way I'd pay any special
attention to it during this delicate period of transition. I pulled
my gaze up, up, up. Good, he was wearing a suit and a tie . . . But
where was his head?! Where was it?! I *can* look past a lot of things
but, my God, marry a headless groom?! I sat there, peering closely,
peering really closely, and I saw something moving around all of a
sudden. Look at thaaaat . . . it was a pair of human eyes! Yes, sirree,
someone's eyes were moving about. But where were the other parts?
I couldn't see a nose or a mouth. The groom's face was basically a
big ball of hair that had sprouted some eyes. His hair, his eyebrows,
his beard, and his moustache were all basically one thick strand
of hair miraculously woven around his head. He'd have reminded
you of those cavemen they told us about in history class. I actually
imagined him getting up and dragging me by my hair to a cave.
Buuuuut, Bride, I thought, calm down and shut up. Are you going
to let a beard and a moustache ruin a marriage for you?! Wise up
and be calm about this! Besides, what's so bad about thick hair?!
Isn't it better than the alternative? Shh, shh, don't be stupid. You
have Amani right in front of you, a great example of what it's like
to settle for the sake of establishing a child-generating partnership!
The height of sacrifice for the sake of future generations!

On either side of the groom, I saw that he'd brought his sisters
along, and one of them was much bubblier than the other. Two
rows of teeth that had grown a woman, basically. It was obvious
the other one had been forced to come. She was glaring at me
like I'd just handed her the electric bill. Ahhh, yes. I know the
type. Either she was still single and thought that every marriage
that took place among humankind was a personal insult to her

(she reminds me of someone, but I can't quite put my finger on it . . . ), or she was in a miserable marriage and thought it was a waste for her brother to make any woman happy. None of my business anyway. To each their own. There was NO WAY I was going to let anyone ruin this. Anyway, that's enough of that because the groom started talking from a place located in the bottom half of his face.

The groom: "Listen, Uncle . . . we're the kind of people who like going about things the right away. And we've heard a lot of good things about you from Mr. Abdel Fattah."

Baba: "From who?"

The groom: "Mr. Abdel Fattah."

Baba: "Who's Mr. Abdel Fattah?!"

The groom: "This guy."

And he pointed toward FouFou, who turned to see who he meant.

FouFou: "Who? Oh, right, right. Me."

The groom: "Obviously, we don't know you directly, but his friend, Brother Emad, is my cousin and he says great things about you. And as far as I'm concerned, I'm prepared to meet all your requests, God willing."

Mama intervened: "That quick?! Don't you want to talk to her and get to know her first?"

"Whaaaat?!" (That would be the two musketeers he'd brought along, shouting in unison and banging their hands against their rib cages, which were about ready to break.)

Mama: "I . . . uh . . . I just mean that they should talk so they can get to know each other."

The groom: "We don't do stuff like that, Hagga. All we care about is a person's upbringing."

His little speech made me happy. No sitting around, and no useless small talk and some more staring at the floor until my neck was ready to crack. Sight-unseen-style . . . maybe that was what was going to work after all.

Mama: "Right, but we should get to know more about
what you're like first . . . I mean, we don't like to get
too conservative."

The groom: "And who does?"

Mama: "Well, as far as her job . . ."

The groom: "It's a very honorable calling, and I don't have
a problem with it."

(I had no idea it was honorable.)

Mama: "Visiting her family . . ."

The groom: "Of course. You have to be good to your family!"

Mama: "Going out and having fun . . ."

The groom: "Of course. I like going out myself, as long as it's
to respectable places."

Mama: "Television and the Internet . . ."

The groom: "As long as I trust in her intelligence, which
I've heard a lot about, then I'm confident in the decisions
she makes."

(How great is this?! This was a full-option groom, people!)

Mama: "Well, as far as finances go . . ."

The groom: "I'm thankful to God that I have a big four-room
apartment with a large living room, and it's fully furnished."

Mama: "That's great . . . I mean, if all goes well, there'll be a
few things we'll need to buy."

The groom: "No, no, things WILL go well, God willing."
(Look at you, Mr. Confidence!) "And, God willing, there won't
be anything we need to buy."

Mama: "Yes, but what about furniture and things for around
the house?"

The groom: "Oh, no, no. Not even those. The apartment
has everything."

Baba: "That's enough, then, Umm Bride; it's obvious that he's
bought everything already, and it's all spanking new. What more
could we ask for?! After everything goes well . . ."

The groom: "Oh, everything is GUARANTEED to go well, God willing." (Unshakeable confidence!) "But, I mean, the furniture isn't really all that new."

Mama started zooming in on him.

Baba: "Oh . . . right. I mean, a bachelor living alone and all. I'm sure he's used the stuff a little bit."

The groom: "No . . . To be honest, that's not really the case."

Baba: "Then what? Have you bought used furniture?"

The groom: "No, no. God forbid. How could I do that to the daughters of good families?!"

Baba: "Then what is the case?"

That was when we heard a car alarm go off on the street.

The groom: "I think that's my car. Is it all right if I go out onto the balcony to turn the alarm off?"

Baba: "Of course. Go ahead."

Out went the groom, with my father on his heels, and FouFou and Amani took off running with Hind behind them because they wanted to nose around and figure out the make of his car. Mama got up to get us some drinks, and I was left alone with the darling sisters in the living room.

All of a sudden, in the blink of an eye, the smile on the bubbly sister's face disappeared, and she gave me the same glare the other sister had given me. I shrank in my seat and my extremities went all aquiver (I'm not too sure what extremities are but all that's important is that they were aquiver). The two of them got up and walked toward me . . . MOMMY! . . . and sat down next to me like the Kasr El-Nil lions,* one on the right and one on the left. And each one zoomed in on one of my ears and leaned over, ready to bite them off. No, no . . . they didn't bite me, but they did whisper reaaaaallly quietly into my ears.

*Large statues located in downtown Cairo.

The first: "Don't go through with the marriage, if you know what's good for you."

The second: "You won't be happy. We want what's best for you."

The first: "He's cut from a different cloth than you are and you won't get along."

The second: "That's beside the fact that there is no way we'll allow him to marry a pharmacist."

The first: "You want to come around and act like you're the bee's knees?!"

Me: "But I'm not a bee."

The first: "Sssshh . . . lower your voice."

The second: "You've got a brain. Use it."

Right then, the others walked in, and the whispering turned into hugs and kisses.

The first: "DAHLING, I've really grown to love you!"

The second: "I swear, you're going to be such a stunning bride!"

The first: "We're going to treat you like a princess!"

Mama didn't like that last comment, and she could tell that I was begging for her to save me via ethereal extra-sensory communication.

Mama: "Wait . . . what? . . . Is your apartment in the family building?"

The groom: "Oh, no, no. My apartment's far away from the family house. I know it's a touchy issue for a lot of people."

Baba: "Well, even if it's in the family building, Umm Bride, so what? The man looks like he comes from a respectable family, from good people; it even shows in the Misses here."

The groom: "Misses?! What Misses?! They have three kids each!"

Baba: "Oh, I apologize! The two Missuses, then! I'm sure we'll get to know them more over time?"

The first: "Well of course we have to get to know each other. Aren't we going to be living with your daughter in the same apartment?"

Mama: "Whaaaat?! What does that mean?! Didn't you say your apartment's far away from where your family lives? How is it your sisters are going to be living with you, then?"

The groom: "You guys think these two are my sisters?"

All of us: "Then what?!"

The groom: "No, no! This is Tahani, my first wife. And this is Amal, my second wife. I'm doing things the orthodox way. There's no way I'd marry another woman without getting my other wives' approval. I mean, naturally. All orthodox."

You know how the Titanic felt when it hit the iceberg? No, of course you don't. Did the Titanic even have feelings? Anyway, just picture something like that . . . We couldn't even find it in ourselves to yell or to object or to trip anyone down the stairs.

Baba: "Go home, son. Go home. Get on your way now. We don't have any girls here who want to get married."

The first: "So they're not getting married?!"

Baba: "No!"

The second: "You swear?!"

Baba: "I said there'll be no marriage!"

The two of them in unison: "Yaaaaaaaaaaaaaaaaaaaaaaaaaaa-aaaaaaaaaaaaaaaaaaaahooo!"

And that was the first time cries of joy filled our humble living room.

# How to Hunt Down a Groom

Well, well, weeelll. You, and that girl, and that one over there are running over here, wanting advice! How am I supposed to come up with advice?! If I had any helpful information, wouldn't I have used it myself?! You people are so strange, I swear. Anyway, the title of this entry is the same as the title of a book they say is on the market these days, and that's been kicking up a giant fuss. Of course, once I heard the name of the book from a friend, the very next second I zipped off to see my boss.

"Excuse me, Dr. Ibtihal . . . I'd like to leave early today."

"Today won't work. There are people coming by to do inspections and no one's leaving early."

"It's not like I'm asking for something illegal! It's my right, guaranteed by the constitution!"

She looked up and glared at me, her entire nervous system on alert, the way bosses have been trained to at the sound of an employee saying anything with the tiniest whiff of politics.

"Excuse me?! Constitution?! Where'd you learn that word from, anyway?"*

"I . . . I . . . I mean, the law. A right guaranteed by the law."

"I said no!"

I figured what the heck? This was worth pulling out the big guns for. I went through my head, trying to find a sad scene. The saddest scenes in my head: Leonardo DiCaprio dying in *Titanic*, when I found out how much I'd be making at my job every month, Karim Abdel Aziz's wedding picture. Yeeeess!! Karim's wedding picture!

*Opponents of Mubarak's regime argue that his thirty-year rule and some of his policies are in violation of the Egyptian constitution. Mention of the constitution is taken as a sign of political activism.

95

"Sniff . . . sniff . . . sniff . . . if you only knew what I'm going through!"

"What you're going through?! What is it, sweetie, what's wrong? Talk to me, I'm like your mother. Is anyone ill? Has there been a death in the family, God forbid?! What is it? Tell me."

"I don't know! . . . I mean . . . I can't tell you! All I can say is that I never would have asked for this if it weren't for the incredibly oppressive situation I'm in."

"But the inspection . . ."

"WAAAAAAAAAAAAAA!!!!!"

"Okay, never mind, never mind! I'll tell you what—given the circumstances you're dealing with, which are clearly incredibly oppressive—you can leave. I'll sort out the half day with the woman in charge of sign-outs, Mrs. Amal."

Before she'd gotten the last letter of the last word out, I had disappeared from the office, and was flying out of the hospital. This was an opportunity I had to seize . . . You know what it's been like for me. And I had as much a chance of getting my hands on a copy of the book as Saad El-Soghayar has of getting a Nobel Prize.

I had to move quickly. The battle was raging and the clock was ticking away; there was no time left to waste! And if this book was the solution . . . then there was no way I was going to let it pass me by.

I ran to 'Am Sobhy, the guy who owns the newspaper stand by the hospital, but as soon as I got there, I ran into two or three doctors I work with. How embarrassing was this?!

I pulled 'Am Sobhy, who knows me because I buy the papers from him every morning, aside:

"Hey, 'Am Sobhy . . ."

"Yes, Doctor?"

"I saw an ad for this book in yesterday's paper . . ."

"What book?"

"This book—I guess it's supposed to be funny, has some jokes and all—is called *How to . . .*"

"*Hunt Down a Groom!*" (He said this loudly enough to be heard by the people standing around.)

"What's going on, 'Am Sobhy?! Are you trying to humiliate me?!"

"No, Doctor, it's just that you're too late. I had two copies left and, because so many people were asking for it, I sent for another twenty-five."

"Well that's good. Give me a copy, then."

"I told you, Doctor, you're too late. The twenty-five copies were sold before they came down from the van."

"What?! Who bought them?"

"The twelve women who work with you in the pharmacy and a bunch of nurses."

"Good God . . . even the nurses can't get themselves married?! The Apocalypse has come, people!"

I left 'Am Sobhy after I heard the two guy doctors asking for copies for their sisters. Why didn't each doctor just marry the other guy's sister, already?! So what if they're already married?! What are friends for? Crazy people. No logic there whatsoever.

I remembered there was a place about three blocks from the hospital that always carried large quantities of books. Whenever I couldn't find a book in the other stores, I always knew I'd find a copy or two there.

"Excuse me, I want to ask about a book . . . not for me or anything . . . it's for a friend of mine."

"For you or for your friend, lady, not like I'm gonna interrogate ya. What's the title?"

"It's called . . . She told me its title but I forget . . . something like *How to Catch . . . How to Get . . . How . . .*"

"*How to Hunt Down a Groom?*"

"Yeah, something like that."

He took out a small notebook and started writing:

"6/2008."

"What?"

"Your number. I'm reserving a copy for you, but sorry, there's a ton of demand. The date could've been even later but you're lucky God fixed up this one lady's luck, and she got engaged and came in and canceled her order."

"Oh really?! And I'm supposed to wait around a whole year?!"

"Lady, all you're doing is waiting around anyway. This isn't going to make much of a difference."

I gathered up what was left of my pride and decided I wasn't going to buy the book. I didn't need to be humiliated by newspaper vendors too. Besides, he was right—if I was going to have to wait a day or two, a year wouldn't make a difference. Okay, enough. No book, no nothing. What could the book possibly say?!

I decided to go home. Close to where I live, I saw a little bookstore with a display of books in the window. My mind started egging me on again: Woman, why don't you just try?! You've got nothing to lose. Maybe you'll find it in this dinky little place. I tried to resist the wild impulse inside of me and, as always, I failed. I walked toward the bookstore, first one foot then the other.

"Excuse me, there's this book that I'm looking for . . . to cut a long story short, it's called *How to Hunt Down a Groom*."

"We have it!"

"What?! . . . Seriously?! You have it?"

I pulled three pounds out of my purse . . . Yes, it's cheap, but maybe it would be the answer.

"Thirty."

"Thirty what? . . . Thirty pounds?! What are you, crazy?! You're making it ten times more expensive?! . . . What kind of racket is this?!"

He gave me a look that meant: You can scream allll day, lady, and I won't pay the slightest bit of attention to you.

I looked at my purse angrily (damn this humiliation!), and I pulled out thirty pounds and handed it to him.

"Dollars."

"Excuse me?"

"Dollaaaaars. Thirty dollars."

"I'm going to call the police! I bet you don't even have the book! Are you cons or something?!"

He reached under a desk and pulled out a copy of the book, wrapped with extreme care in layers of cellophane.

I was speechless and I was mesmerized and I was stupefied. There it was! There was the solution! Who would've believed that the solution to the marriage problem would be in a book?! Couldn't they have released it under the Reading Is for Everyone campaign?* At the least it would be more useful than anything else they've released. It would solve Egyptian society's problem! I was reaching my hand out for the book when I heard a car screech to a halt outside, and I saw a woman get out and leave it in the middle of the road. The woman was running like she was in the middle of a marathon; she jumped, and all of a sudden she was in the middle of the store, clutching onto the hand of the man who was holding the book.

The woman: "What is this?! Were you going to sell it?! I got you the twenty dollars! Didn't I tell you I was going to buy some currency and come right back?!"

The bookstore owner: "This lady here is paying thirty."

The woman turned to me, panicked: "Thirty?! You're paying thirty?!"

Me: "I . . ."

She turned away from me.

The woman: "I KNEW you were going to do this, so I planned for it! Here's thirty dollars."

*Campaign established by Egypt's First Lady, Susan Mubarak.

The bookstore owner: "But I think the lady might pay more . . ."

The woman turned and grabbed onto my hand: "I beg you! . . . I beg you! You don't know what I'm going through! I have four daughters, and if they don't get married before they're thirty, I'm going to DIE! I beg you! Don't you have a mother?! I beg you, let me have the copy, and give me your phone number, and when I'm done marrying off the four girls, I'll call you and sell you the book."

Good God . . . I still have to wait for you to marry off FOUR girls?! The 6/2008 date would be sooner! But was I seriously going to pay thirty dollars?! Where was I supposed to find a currency dealer at that hour?! . . . The woman really did remind me of Mama, and in light of the emerging conditions and the dollar crisis in the country, I had no option but to let the book go. And so off ran the woman to her car, yelling in victory:

"Wheeeeee!! Wheeeee!!! Wheeeeeee!! Wheeeeeee!!"

(The mothers have lost it, people.)

So, from this place and from the position I inhabit, I send an appeal to anyone who has bought the book: a copy for your little sister here . . . fine, fine, don't get fussy . . . your much, much older sister. Bliss and rewards will be for those who do good deeds!

# A-Hunting We Go!

So what did I do? After I failed to get a hold of *the* book, I decided to establish HHAG (that stands for How to Hunt a Groom—don't you start thinking it's something else!), a group of delightful young women in similar circumstances, with which you are all too familiar. Anyway, we split ourselves up into subgroups: one subgroup was responsible for looking for the book, another for milking information from women with successful marriages, and one to call the police . . . Woops, I mean, to tally the information we gathered and summarize it in a way that was easy to understand, so then maybe WE'd be able to publish a book.

Now this whole thing was really getting to me. I was plunging into it with all my extremities . . . the ones I am aware of and the ones I am not. I went on another search mission for the book, but without the slightest glimmer of hope. Came back having found neither hide nor hair of it (cultured people out there should get ready for me to ask them what this hair or hide business is). I was this far away from developing chronic defeatedness as well as a case of seasonal depression of the severe variety. It is totally obvious that I'm a failure at this marriage thing. But to be a failure at finding a *book* that explained how to get married . . . well, that was just too much! I told myself it was best to get out of the first subgroup and join the second, where something could actually happen.

You guys, all I really need is for someone to say, "Work at it, Bride," and I'll work at it forever. I mean, I'm smart and I'm sharp and I get the gist of things in a snap. It's just that my brain gets rusty and won't work when it comes to this marriage business. It needs a bit of polishing up. And all the time, all they'll say to me is "chin up, chin up." And I don't know *how* to pull my chin up. If someone could just tell me how, I'd pull my chin up forever.

So I told myself that the only thing left for me to do was to ask "people of experience," and that it had to be family first. I'd start with mine . . . maybe . . .

It turns out that I said the above tirade out loud . . . and in front of my grandmother.

"Holy Lord . . . have you lost your mind or something, Bride?!"

"No, Teita, I haven't lost my mind or anything."

"No, you can tell me. Don't be scared. I said it a long time ago, the minute my boy wanted to marry *that woman*—your mother, that is—I said, 'She looks like she's off her rocker, and she's going to give you some crazy children.'"

"Mama is not crazy, Teita; she's the best! Who's as good as she is?!"

"Yeah, yeah. And who sticks up for the bride?!"

"No, Teita, no! Don't say that word in front of me. It's given me a complex."

"A complex?! I told my son ages ago, when he was about to marry *that woman*—your mother, that is—I said, 'She's messed up, and she's going to pop out some messed up kids for you.'"

"Siiiiiigh. Teita, I told you, Mama's the best! Besides, she's smart as a button. At least she managed to land a catch as great as Baba . . . don't you think?"

"Of course! Your dad is a gem! Now your *mother* . . ."

"Hmmm?!"

"Is great too! Just great . . . She gave birth to some kids, at least. But tell me, why do you say you have a complex now? Destiny comes in the blink of an eye!"

"Destiny just doesn't want to come around, Teita. I don't know if it's walking from Halayeb,* or what's taking it so long. Tell me,

*An Egyptian city near the border with Sudan, and a considerable distance from Cairo.

Teita, how did you get married? I mean, did you do something that made Geddo fall for you, or what?"

"Sshh, girl, don't be rude!"

"Oh please, Teita, give me some advice. I'm a failure at things like this!"

"Even though your mother herself was entirely *too* good at things like this . . . Anyway, sweetie, no man *wants* to get married. Someone has to push him. His mother, his sisters, and if it's neither, it has to be the bride herself."

"Check you out, Teita! Even better with age!"

"Naturally . . . just ask me. A long time ago, I was . . . oh the good ol' days! . . . I rocked my world back then."

"Thaaaat's what I'm looking for. *How* did you rock it?! Explain it to me, for the love of God!"

"Listen, I'm going to give you some advice. But this is between you and me. Don't go and tell anyone and ruin my reputation with the rest of the family!"

"Ooh, this is obviously risqué business! Give me that advice, Teita!"

"I was beautiful. The most beautiful girl in the neighborhood."

"Hmm, you wouldn't think it."

"What?! What're you saying? Speak louder!"

"Nothing, nothing. I said, 'Obviously.'"

"Yes. I used to go out on the balcony to fill the water jugs, and I'd linger around and the whole street would go crazy. And that night, four suitors would go see my father!"

"That's it?! You'd go out and dandy around and fill jugs?!"

"And you think that was a small thing?! I used to linger and hang my braids, which were the color of gold, out the window, and they'd fly around with every puff of wind and, honestly, we just had a lot of jugs to fill."

"Well, what are people like us, who don't have any jugs, supposed to do?!"

"Supposed to do? Supposed to do? I don't know, sweetie. It's true, you're a poor little generation with no jugs."

My tante Fadya, because of her hobby of standing at doors "polishing doorknobs," heard the conversation:

"You're teaching the girl about jugs, Mama?! Listen, Bride, lovey, *I* had a foolproof method."

"Okay . . ."

"I had this little red miniskirt and these high boots, and you know what men are like with red. I'd take two steps down our street, all quiet like, and, bit by bit, buy something from here . . . and something from there. Get in a taxi, get out of a taxi. Mill around, in other words. At night, five suitors would be meeting with my dad!"

"All at once?!"

"At once! What'd you think brought your uncle around?!"

"Well, Tante, what about women who don't wear miniskirts, red or any other color, what're they supposed to do?!"

"Supposed to do? Supposed to do? I swear, I have no idea. It's true, you're a poor little generation with no miniskirts."

"Fantastic! I can get nothing useful out of you two. I should go to Amani's daughter, Hind, right now. Maybe I can get something I can actually use from *her.*"

"Hold on, sweetie, where you going?! Your Tante Raqya is the only solution! Now she, in particular, has to have at least a million methods! Do you know how many suitors she had?!"

"Quantity doesn't matter; it's all about quality! Besides, all that's important is that plans actually materialize."

"Don't worry. She's the one who'll know what needs to be done."

And so we called Tante Raqya. It took her a while to come to the phone because her son had just swallowed a nail, and her husband was in a cast because she'd busted two of his ribs when she was "joking around" with him in the middle of a little tiff, and her daughter was standing on the balcony and insisting on jumping off

like Spiderman . . . totally successful marriage Tante Raqya has
going. She'd be the one to tell me what needed to be done, all right.

Tante Raqya came to the phone:

"Listen, honey, I've wanted to have a talk with you for ages.
So here's some solid advice for you. Men are like drums: empty
on the inside, and you have to give them a good beating to get
any sound out."

"What does that mean?!"

"Look, you do what I did with your uncle Mohsen. Pick a guy
you like and follow him on the street."

"Hit on him, you mean?"

"Where's your brain, girl?! No, have *him* hit on *you.*"

"Like . . . force him to?"

"How are you this stupid?! No, sweetie, just get in front of him,
then turn around and—bam!"

"Bam?"

"Give him a slap so big it'll leave his ears ringing for a week!"

"But he could slap me back! Am I supposed to get humiliated
and slapped on the street?!"

"Impossible! As soon as a man sees a woman's hand about to
land loudly on his cheek, his life changes *completely*!"

"Oh yeah?!"

"Of course! Stupid people will tell you that the way to a man's
heart is through his stomach . . . nonsense! The way to a man's
heart begins with a single step . . . your hand leaving a mark
on his cheek . . . How else have your uncle and I been living in
happiness for nine years?!"

"How's his arm, by the way? When's he getting the cast off?"

"Soon, God willing. Can't believe that happened. Weaklings
those men are!"

"Well, then what, Tante? I smack him, he proposes?!"

"No, silly. After you smack him, you turn around and call
over a police constable and say: 'This man was hitting on me;

drag him off to the station!' And the guy will get scared and will choose proposing over jail."

"You mean I should blackmail him and make him marry me by force?!"

"Are you going to get all conscientious on me?! Nothing else works with men! Take it from someone who's got experience."

"But what if there isn't a police constable around? . . . What do constables look like, anyway? I've never seen one in my entire life."*

"No constable? No constable? Now *that* is one thing I did not take into consideration. Back in my day, there was always a constable. God help you. You're a poor little generation with no constables."

I tried as hard as I could to follow their instructions. I couldn't find any jugs, but I gathered up all the potted plants and sat on the balcony, watering them, and nothing happened. I couldn't put on a miniskirt, but I did buy a pair of red boots and walk around on our street from freaking dawn until the end of the day, till my feet got blistered all over, and STILL, nothing happened. I walked down the street and then turned around so I could slap the person behind me, but before I could even raise my arm, he'd pulled out a knife and stolen my cell phone. Oh, if only there was a constable . . . but what can you do?! It's just our luck . . . poor generation with no constables.

In sum, all of the pieces of advice failed miserably. Or maybe my luck is what failed miserably . . .

That's not a maybe, actually . . . that's a certainty!

After the first meeting of the Grand HHAG Egyptian United Socialist Group, and after all the information the members had gathered from families and friends, and the Internet to boot,

---

*Until the middle of the twentieth century, constables were positioned in streets throughout Egypt for the purpose of protecting residents—particularly women—from unbecoming or dangerous behavior; street constables are no longer a part of Egyptian life, where sexual harassment has been on the rise.

had been tallied, and after implementing some of the pieces of advice, most of which failed miserably, and after failing to get a single copy of the fated book, we decided to make our first meeting our last. To each citizen their own.

Keep in mind, of course, that the cursed will always be cursed . . . even if good luck smacks them across the face.

# The Eighth

YAAAAAAAY!!! I've got a suitor!! Surprised? Not that I've got a suitor, obviously, you guys know I've had piles upon piles of them at my place. What's surprising is that I'm *happy* that I've got a suitor, especially since the last three or four grooms had me about ready to collapse from an existential crisis and a nervous breakdown. But what am I supposed to do, you guys? I have a kind heart and I don't hold grudges! Mama, especially, tries to take advantage of the whole kindheartedness thing:

"Well, so *what* if Auntie-Body got you a horrible groom once? She might aim right the next time . . . And so what if, instead of finding you a groom, Amani got you a whole big, happy family?! God knows what's possible next time! Invite Auntie-Body over for lunch. And go on a little walk and visit Amani. Turn on the stairwell light for her husband, FouFou, because he's scared of the dark. And it would be great if you could shoo the cats away for him too. Help Amani out, the woman has to go down to escort him up the stairs every day."

My kind heart aside, I'm stubborn as heck, and my pride kicks in big time. It's not easy for me to invite Auntie-Body over for lunch unless we've cooked rice topped with nuts and sprinkled with some of that Abido powder you use to kill roaches. But I said, "Fine . . . of course . . . God willing . . . God help us."

People who are knee-deep in the whole living-room meet-ups thing and who have experience related to the topic will know that grooms come, according to the laws of nature and the Islamic prayer tradition, in unison. Bam, bam, bam—five suitors in a go. And they show up, one after the other, and they stink . . . total losers . . . nothing there . . . "How did THAT happen?!" . . . "Was he in an accident or does his head just look like that?!" . . . And the party comes to an end on that note. And then, aaaaaageeees go by without a peep. Nobody comes anywhere near our door, and Baba has to call the electrician over just to make sure that our doorbell's still working, in case they have been coming after all and we aren't hearing them ring the bell. In the down period, the three senses a girl uses to figure out if she's getting a suitor or not get stronger.

The sense of hearing: A girl opens her ears up way wide anytime her mother's on the phone and says: "She's good, thank you for asking." Followed by: "Still." And that ever-present cliché: "She's met a lot but her destiny hasn't come around yet." Because anyone who talks about a topic like that on the phone is pretty likely to be prepping for something . . . or sometimes, the person is just being condescending.

The sense of sight: A girl visually sweeps every area she's in, especially her work environment. Anytime she spots an older woman with a guy who looks like he could be her son staring at her from far away, she flips on her other channel, plugs in the girlie wires, adjusts the antenna, and forces the neck muscles into placing the head at a ninety degree angle from the rest of the body in a sign of good manners and perfect breeding.

The sense of smell: Also used at work, or even when a girl's walking in or out of her building. Important because of the custom that dictates that suitors desiring to marry must bathe in half a bottle of cologne or aftershave. The cologne thing is the replacement for the olden days' squeaky shoe, another device that would let a bride know somebody was following her on the street, inspiring her to take forty-five minutes to walk down a path that usually takes five.

Anyway, after I recharged all these senses . . . nothing. Absolutely nothing was happening. I left it all up to God. There was nothing else I could do. I started thinking seriously about inviting Auntie-Body over for lunch and about helping Amani and FouFou with the staircase and cats issue. But God sent me divine rescue in the form of Umm Mahrous.

Now Umm Mahrous is the main source of dairy products in our area. You get the feeling that the woman's got her head on straight, despite the fact that she only has one eye and that she always wears a black *galabeyya* and has a bit of Negmah Ibrahim in her.* She always says that she's taken up the dairy thing as a hobby, something to pass the time with now that her husband has three auto rickshaws that bring in good money. But Umm Mahrous considers bringing people together to be her true calling. Telling the family in one apartment what the family in another apartment is up to, telling the people in this building the scandals going on in that building. Ever since she and Mama met, my mother has thought of her as the best invention humanity has known since the Internet . . . maybe even better. The Internet can't help you make rice pudding.

One day, on my way back from work, I saw something that touched me deeply: Mama hugging Umm Mahrous while the two of them wept so intensely it would've tugged at your heartstrings (what ARE heartstings?!). Mama was sobbing like there was no tomorrow, and Umm Mahrous looked like she was clutching some of the money that Mama hides from Baba behind the electric meter.

"What's wrong, Mama? Why are you crying?!"

"It's just . . . it's just . . . Ohhh."

And Mama pulled me into a group hug with the two of them that could have beat what that clever lady from the Oprah show does. Inside the apartment, I let it rip:

*Egyptian actress known for her chilling portrayal of one of Egypt's most infamous female criminals. A *galabeyya* is a traditional dresslike garment worn by both men and women in the Middle East.

"Umm Mahrous?! It's come to Umm Mahrous?!"

"What's wrong with Umm Mahrous?! We've tried neighbors and friends, and it didn't work. Maybe God will . . ."

"You just said it yourself: All the respectable, cultured people we know turned out to be just like the People's Assembly. All promises in the beginning and all scandals in the end. So how can you think that Umm Mahrous will be the solution?! . . . Mama!"

And I walked off toward my room. Halfway there, I froze when I thought I heard something unusual:

"What? I think I heard you say something?"

"Oh reeeaaally?! *Now* you want to listen . . . When you hear that she's brought you a *doctor* who has his own *clinic*."

"Well that's not really important, Mama . . . It's the person himself that matters! It's not like I'm going to marry a clinic, now am I?!"

"Oh, you'd marry a hair salon! Let me tell you . . . I'm tired. So tired."

"Okay, okay. I'll marry the clinic . . . I mean, I'll meet the groom! What else do I have to do?!"

"That's more like it! Wise up!"

Anyway, after that, Mama went on an investigative tour so that she could gather as much information as possible about the groom before he graced our respectable living room. So we wouldn't be surprised and end up finding out that he had two wives, or was from Riyadh, or did celebrity impersonations. Mama gathered all the information she could, but she still wasn't satisfied. After all the disasters that had taken place in our living room, and especially after the trills of joy from Mr. Brown Sandals' family last time around, Mama decided to do things differently. She came up with an idea that I really liked, to be honest: *we* would go to see the groom!

Right after Mama got the address of the clinic from Umm
Mahrous, she let us know that he was expecting us. Mama got
really ticked off:

"Why would you *do* that, woman?!"

Umm Mahrous's genius answer:

"Well, so he can get ready for the meeting too!"

(Justice will prevail! Justice will prevail!)

Finally, the tables were turned, and *he* would be the one who'd
wait for *us*. How awesome is that, that he'd turn the clinic upside
down, pull up the legs of his pants, get down on all fours to mop
the floor with his receptionist?! He'd beat the rugs and dust the
curtains, and stand in front of the closet, torn: Should I wear this
shirt or that one? Should I spike my hair up or part it on the side?
And he'd get us something cold to drink and a dozen pieces of
gâteaux. Ohhhh yes! I'd finally be eating gâteaux that hadn't cost
my dad a fortune and that he wouldn't be using to make me feel
guilty when it turned out that he'd bought them all for nothing.

Here we go, Bri-Bri, I thought, You have to play this right.
I put on a chic suit and these great brown sandals (why can't I
wear brown sandals too?!), and Mama put on a nice outfit and
all the gold that we knew she had as well as all the gold that she
keeps hidden in the secret safe under the clothes rack for God-
knows-what emergencies. And boy, did I play the role all right.

"He has to be fair skinned and have yellow eyes and silky
green hair and a deep voice, and he has to honor marital life and
he has to contribute to buying the furniture . . . and he has to be
perfect from all angles. And may God smite down anyone who
doesn't praise the Lord!"

We went to the building with the clinic in it. It had a
huuuuuuge sign with his name on it, and as soon as the doorman
saw us, he got up and escorted us up in a symphony of respect,
all the way to the door of the clinic. Mama had decided that
even if the clinic was cricket-chirping empty and didn't bring

in anything more than fifty pounds a month to our brother-citizen-groom, she'd *still* marry me off to him and she'd support us financially herself, if it meant getting rid of the back-crippling load represented by my esteemed presence. Do you *see* how classy she is?! Mama was ready to sacrifice mother and child so that the doctor and I could live!

As soon as we walked in and introduced ourselves to the receptionist, he jumped up with a start that was just like the doorman's, and he went in to announce to the groom that we'd arrived. The patients—there were so many they filled the clinic—all turned to each other and whispered: "That's her! That's her!" What was going on here, people?! I am quite the catch . . . but this was too much. The receptionist led us in even though Mama was insisting on waiting until the doctor had seen all his patients (it would all go toward my wedding jewelry anyway), but the man insisted on letting us in first, and none of the patients objected. Would you look at that?! Such good people! If it weren't for the fact that they would be putting food on our table every month, I'd say, "God give them good health!"

Anyway, we walked into the office. Chic desk and walls with so many certificates hanging on them I thought it had to have taken twenty years for someone to earn them all . . . I *had* forgotten to ask how old he was. It was obvious he was older, but by how much? I walked in with my eyes half closed. I was scared I'd be stunned again. But this time, I was prepared. I'd wanted to bring some walnuts and some almonds and have him crack them to make sure he had strong teeth, but then I remembered they only brought walnuts and almonds for *women*.* That it was a girlie thing, in other words. So I'd brought him some *doums*.† The true test of a man's

---

*An obsolete practice where a suitor's mother would test the strength of a potential bride's teeth by asking her to crack open nuts.

†The fruit of *Hyphaene thebaica*, a type of palm tree native to the Nile region; *doums* are small, circular fruits with a hard exterior reminiscent of acorns.

teeth! If he turned out to be like the suitor before him, I'd pelt the
*doums* at his noggin and nobody would be able to blame me . . . I'm
not a doormat, people!

Mama put her hand out to shake his and poked me so I'd do
the same. I said my *bismillah*, pulled my eyes up, and found . . . an
amazing specimen of humanity! All the characteristics I was just
talking about: green eyes and light brown hair, tall and broad
and high. He flashed a little smile that showed off his dimples.
Ewwwwwww. What was this, then?! Was I going to marry a man
who was prettier than me?! I'd sit next to him at the wedding and
people would say, "What'd he marry *her* for?!" . . . Not agaaaaain.
You have to look past these faults, Bride, I thought. We're not
going to hold people's looks against them. It's not his fault he's cute
and is one volt away from lighting up, as El-Limby says.* Fine,
fine. I'd suck it up and marry him. Besides, he did have a flaw. He
had this little scar on his forehead shaped like a star. It looked like
he had been a troublemaker when he was younger. Good. At least
I wasn't getting a pansy.

We sat down and asked for soft drinks. Heeey, where was
the gâteaux?! Was it only a divinely ordained duty for brides'
families, or what? A while after we sat down, the guy turned
around in his chair and sat there, looking at me. I don't like this
googly-eyed business. I needed to bring out the *doums*. They'd
set the situation straight. He and my mom talked, and the
whole time he was talking to Mama, he was looking at me and
focusing really intently. It got so intense my temperature went
up, and my nerves were shot to heck, and my hand reacted with
the cold drink I was holding to form a layer of steam that added
a terribly romantic touch to the atmosphere. Despite the fact
that I'm a new model that's just hit the market, with automatic
locks, seat belts, and an anti-googly-eyes mechanism, my nerves

*Character in an Egyptian movie known for outlandish one-liners.

couldn't withstand it all. THAT'S IT. STOOOOP. HE'S
THE ONE! ALL DONE HERE! There wasn't a single thing
wrong with him. You were patient, and you were rewarded,
Bri-Bri. Wheee!!! The kids in the pharmacy were going to *die*.
A *doctor*, with a *clinic*, and *dimples*. It was going to be so sweet at
my wedding, my friends about ready to explode! Or . . . no, no.
No evil daydreams. Leave the smugness and the gloating to
somebody else . . . somebody with an engagement ring from a
doctor on her finger. Hehehehe.

We made it through the two-hour visit, during which Mama
dragged out all the necessary information, and during which I
didn't hear a single word either of them said. It was like I was
watching a silent movie with my eyes wide open and the rest of my
senses canceled out. We walked out of the clinic positively flying.
We'd taken so long the waiting area was empty when we came
out. Mama got really embarrassed and apologized to the doctor:

"It looks like we took a long time and the patients got sick
of waiting."

"No, ma'am, don't worry about it at all. They'll come back."

"Why?"

"They don't trust anyone else but me. Where would they go?
They'll go round and round and come right back. And even if
they don't come back, it doesn't matter! What matters is that I
got to meet you, ma'am. That's more important than a hundred
prescriptions and two hundred patients!"

(You're all familiar with what the word "ma'am" does to the
women in our family.)

Mama left in disbelief. She was leaning on me because she
was so happy she was dizzy. I couldn't believe it myself either. As
we were walking out, we saw his car in front of the building, a
brand new silver Lancer. Look at that, Baba, your salary will be
all yours again! Your money is blessed after all! Mama, in crazed

happiness, spent all she had on me. We bought a new outfit, shoes, a bag, and every time we'd walk into a store, she'd say:

"We want the best you have! She's getting engaged soon! Give us the most expensive thing you've got. Something worthy of a woman who's getting engaged soon!"

"Mama, don't jinx this!"

"No, God willing. God willing, no jinxing!"

Mama bought me the outfit and the bag and the shoes, and we went home. A couple of hours after we got back, the doorbell rang and it was Umm Mahrous, dancing with happiness and jumping around like a frog in a frying pan (She is quite a good dancer, really. She had a bit of Nadia El-Guindy in *Hit and Run in Tel Aviv* going on).* She was there to give Mama the good news that the groom was asking for permission to come over the next Tuesday, which was a week away. He wanted us to know that he was ready for all our requests and that he thought we were a respectable family and that he'd never find anyone better.

Mama got on the phone and began her sacred duty as mother of the bride, which was to gloat to all the women of our honorably family who hadn't found out the news yet:

"God willing, you'll be hearing some good news soon . . . We'll be seeing you soon. All good, all good, God willing . . . It looks like I'll need your help soon. For what? You'll find out soon. No, no, I won't tell you. Let it be a surprise!"

Well, why not me too?! I wanted to gloat—I mean, to talk—to someone too. We had lunch and I went in to take a nap . . . but I couldn't. It was like I was rolling over hot coals, as Fayza Ahmed says . . . or was it Asmahan?† I was rolling over, in any case.

---

*Egyptian actress known for her portrayal of violent, lusty characters.
†The Egyptian singer Fayza Ahmed and the Syrian-Egyptian singer and actress Asmahan were well known in the mid-twentieth century for their songs of idealized love and patriotism.

What's the point of getting engaged if a girl can't gloat—I mean, talk—about it with someone?! No, no, no. This was unbearable! I wanted to go out on the balcony and scream at everyone coming and going: I'M GEEETTTING MAAAAARRIIIIEEEDD!!!!!!!

Okay, okay, that's enough of a tangent. I had to tell someone; I couldn't keep it in . . . I was going to die. Should I go tell Amani? No, no, she's the jealous type and she'll say: "He's *nothing* in comparison to FouFou's brother LouLou." And then I might get impulsive and tell her what I *really* think of her husband and his brother and their whole family, and then her feelings might get a boo-boo or something. Should I go tell Abd Rabbou, the doorman, and rub it in the way he rubs in news about his wife, Queen Soha, anytime he catches a glimpse of me? No, no, I couldn't deal with Soha. She might come up to say congratulations and chew my arm off or something . . . One time, she was happy because our neighbor, Mahmoud Salwa, had graduated high school and gotten into med school, and another time it looked like she got a bit too hungry because we couldn't find a trace of the guava tree and the two kittens that used to fall asleep under it.

Well, should I tell the girls at work? No, no. In case they get all nosy and poke around and figure out where the clinic is and possibly try to visit and snatch him away from me. No, no, no! I had to be smarter than that . . . But who could I tell?! Who!"

I jumped up and got dressed and made up my mind to go visit Noha. I couldn't delay the gloating—I mean, the talking—for another day. I just couldn't. Riding in the taxi, I figured I'd try saying it out loud for the first time:

"Quickly please, driver, my fiancé is waiting for me!"

"No problem, bride!"

Ohhh yeah! What a fabulous word . . . even if under different circumstances I would've yelled, "That's DOCTOR Bride to you." But right then, that label was the best label in the whole world. Down with college degrees!

I arrived at the pharmacy where Noha works evenings. As soon as she saw me, she got all jittery and her face turned yellow. I looked around and saw that the pharmacy was gleaming and that all the shelves had been cleaned. I looked at what she was wearing . . . and my heart sank.

"What's going on with that outfit? . . . You don't wear that outfit unless . . . unless . . . you're meeting a groom!"

"No, that's not true."

"No, there's no way you can fool me! I know that outfit well."

"The outfit . . . the outfit . . . oh, what the heck . . . I *knew* you'd know. Yes, a groom is on his way to meet me."

"He better not be a doctor who has a clinic . . . We don't want a repeat of the Ayman situation."

"No, no. This guy's a pilot. He's coming to see me today. Wait, what's this about Ayman?! What did he do?"

"Ayman . . . I-I-I . . . no, I hope he's fine and well in Benghazi! Anyway, is that why you're trying to blow me off? For the pilot?"

"It's not about blowing you off, Bride. But, what if he came and saw you here? What if he ended up liking you more or something? You wouldn't cramp your sister's style, would you?!"

Ahhhh! It was a good idea, really. He'd show up and I'd pop out all of a sudden, and he'd fall for me and leave the evil Noha chick who wanted to screw me over. And, clearly, there were no similarities between what she was doing and what I had done . . . Ayman?! . . . Ayman had advanced astigmatism and chronic farsightedness! . . . How happy would Mama be if I came home with another groom?! Oh how sweet, Bride! Underdog's luck! A doctor AND a pilot in one week! Oh, you're going to be thrilled, Mama.

. . . Noha looked like she could tell what I was thinking.

"Bride, I'm your *friend* and you love me and there's no way you'd do this to me. You *know* what my luck has been like!"

"Like my luck has been so much better?!"

"I'm sorry, Bride . . . for my sake . . . I know you don't have the heart to do this to me. And I promise I'll make him set you up with one of his friends."

I was just about to sympathize with her when that last line drove me nuts. It had come to this?! I thought: This is happening to me right when I'm about to give you a mouthful and rub your face in the news of *my* groom?! But still, I wasn't about to do anything bad to a friend of mine. Try and steal her groom?! No, no, and no! Besides, the last time around, Ayman had been about ready to have a nervous breakdown and I had been about ready to be thrown into Kanater Prison in a case of ashtray assault. Thank God it had turned out all right. After Noha begged for a while, I decided to go into the lab and wait there. She was my friend, after all, and I didn't have the heart to hurt her. Besides, I had a groom *and* his clinic. No shortage of grooms here!

Right when I was about to give Noha the shock of a lifetime with my news (After adequate mental preparation, of course. Noha's my giiirl and I could never shock her without adequate mental preparation), she was the one who had stunned me and left me standing there feeling like a car full of explosives. Ready to blow up at her there in the pharmacy and at the groom too if I got to see him. Sigh. Like the saying goes, what goes around comes around. Damn you, Noha. You're making me speak in proverbs!

A little bit later, a woman burst into the pharmacy looking so happy she was about to explode. As soon as she saw me, she wiped the smile off her face, so I gathered right away that she was the matchmaker. I know all about the type. Start off all smiley and end up screwing you over and getting pushed down the stairs.

"All right, all right. You don't need to look so grumpy . . . I'm leaving."

I walked down the street, the markings of shock etched on
my once joyful face. (Siiigh. There goes more fancy talk.) So I
couldn't even act smug in front of anyone about my groom?!
I mean, if I went and told everyone at work and then Noha went
and told them her news too, whose story was going to win?
The pilot wins, of course! Besides, it was October. It was the
season for pilots.* First air show at 2:00 p.m. and all that jazz.
What kind of engagement starts off like this?! What's the point
of being engaged if people don't send bad vibes your way and get
jealous, and what's the point if their blood pressure doesn't rise
anytime a girl talks about her fiancé in front of them?! God, why
is there always something missing when I'm happy?!

The week passed by normally. The whole time at work, Noha
and I were giving each other surreptitious looks. Neither of us
wanted to talk about what was going on on our end and neither
of us wanted to ask the other about what was going on on hers.
The whole thing had become a competition and we were waiting
to see who was going to win.

So the week passed by okay and the fateful day arrived: the
groom walked into our humble living room that Mama had
renovated almost completely during the week. New curtains, a
new vase, new cups, everything brand spanking new. As soon
as the groom dude walked in, it was like it was daytime all of a
sudden. I love people who look like they have just stepped out of
the shower! We sat together for a long time, and we talked and
we laughed, and the groom said he couldn't wait to get engaged
and that there was no reason to delay things since everything
we needed was ready. And when Mama and Baba asked about
the family that he'd come without, he said his parents were
in the Emirates and that, God willing, they'd be here for the

---

*October 6 marks the commemoration of the Egyptian victory over Israel in the 1973
Arab-Israeli War.

engagement party. And if they couldn't make it, it was okay; we didn't have to stop sailing ships for something as small as that.

Of course not! Why on earth would we delay things?! That could mean having that sneak of a girl called Noha getting engaged before me and gobbling up all the attention!

After the meeting, I could tell from the look in my mother's eyes that she wasn't comfortable, and in vain—and I repeat, *in vain*—I tried to convince her to get the nagging doubts out of her head. But Mama, because of all the experience she has when it comes to me, had an unjustifiable feeling that there had to be a cloud to every one of my silver linings. So she got on the phone *again*, not to gloat this time, but to get to the root of things and to quiet down the suspicious bees that were buzzing around in her head about the groom in shining armor.

The next day I went to work. Noha still hadn't said anything. Good. Hopefully my thing would turn out okay and Mama wouldn't ruin it . . . Mothers! If they can't find a problem, they make one up!

I got home, and I glanced around the living room and found Mama holding onto the phone exactly the same way she had been when I'd left her fourteen and a half hours earlier. But there was a strange expression on her face.

"What is it, Mama? What's wrong?"

"Oh, it's nothing. Just something your tante Fetna told me when I was gloating—I mean, talking—to her about this groom situation."

"What thing, Mama? You know, I think you've gotten used to having me around and your subconscious is trying to wreck this for me."

"You don't understand . . . Tante Fetna said she knows him and that he's married with kids! Go get changed. We're going to his clinic!"

"What? No, this is *not* fair! We're going to go through the Brown Sandals family thing again?!"

"That's why I'm telling you to get changed quick. I can't wait another second before I find out what exactly is going on!"

We went to the clinic *again*. The Lancer was in its place. The doorman was sleeping next to the door. We went up to the clinic. The receptionist . . . no, it was another guy. Normal enough. This was the nighttime shift, and I'm sure the staff changes around. The patients didn't greet us like they did last time. Fine, now my conscience would be okay with me praying they wouldn't get better. How could they not greet us like they did the first time?! We took our turn and walked in to see the doctor. We waited. And waited. And waited. Until the stranger who was sitting inside the doctor's office with us looked like he had lost his patience as well:

"Which one of you is sick?!"

"Neither one of us is sick."

"Then why are you here?!"

"This is a family matter."

"How is this a family matter?"

"It's between us and the doctor."

"But I'm the doctor!"

(Well, well, well . . . Say it louder, brother, let me hear you say it!)

"No, sir. This is Dr. ——'s clinic."

"I know! I *am* Dr. ——."

"But how?! Dr. —— is younger and he has green eyes and he has . . ."

"Dimples. Isn't that right?"

"Yes! Exactly! Don't tell me he's training with you and that he's still a student and . . ."

The man got up and ran out of the room.

"Mama . . . what is going on?! Is he calling the police to come arrest us or something?"

"What for, the police?! It's not like we've stolen anything . . . Either way, get ready to make a run for it."

Mr. Big Doctor came back, dragging Mr. Small Doctor behind him, who was wearing sweatpants and looking like he'd just been woken up.

"This is him, isn't it?"

"Yes, yes, that's Dr. ——. Have you kidnapped him or something?"

All of a sudden, Mr. Big Doctor started beating up Mr. Small Doctor.

"Kidnapped him?! I wish I could set him on *fire*! . . . Chop him up into pieces! . . . I wish I could throw him off a tower and get rid of him!"

And because we have such kind hearts and because we couldn't understand what was going on, we stood there trying to separate them and screaming. Trying to separate them and screaming. And in the end, Mr. Small Doctor took off running, and Mr. Big Doctor sat down in front of us, a total wreck. We got him some lemonade and told the patients and the receptionist to go home, and he sat there, venting to us about it all.

Get a load of this: the good sir, Mr. Small Doctor with the dimples . . . is his son. The good sir did horribly on his high school exams. His father made him take them again. He still did horribly. He got into a private university where he spent six years but couldn't graduate. He transferred to business school. He'd been there for five years and still had one to go. And because he's the son of a famous doctor and because he's cute and because he has money, he'd taken up messing with people as a hobby. He'd pulled the same charade he pulled on us on a ton of women. On doctors and pharmacists and dentists. He'd make the same grand entrance, show off his clinic and his car, and tell them his mama and baba were in the Emirates but were happy as clams, and he'd show them a letter from them giving their approval.

And he'd get engaged and go out and have fun and live it up and get invited places, and after that they'd find him out or he'd get bored or he'd get a good beating or people would show up at the clinic, ready to destroy his father, and he'd disappear for a couple months and then do it all over again.

*That's* why the certificates on the wall looked like they had taken twenty years to earn . . . they were his father's. *That's* why the patients knew who we were as soon as we walked in . . . they were his friends. *That's* why he'd turned to Umm Mahrous . . . everyone else knew all about his reputation from his friends and his family, and she was still new to the place and hadn't gotten a chance to learn about his scandals. *That's* why he had a scar on his forehead . . . an "understanding" relative of one of the brides had left him a little souvenir to remind him that girls aren't PlayStations.

We calmed Mr. Big Doctor down . . . He was like an old friend at that point, after all, and we had to stand by him. We left and went down to the street like everything was nooormaaal . . . nooormaaal . . . totally normaaaal, I'm telling you. We'd gotten used to this. We weren't holding back tears and we didn't feel sorry for ourselves and we didn't hate the world and all that was in it and I wasn't thinking about Noha, who was probably putting her ring on that very minute, or anything . . . Noooormaaaall.

The next day, I went to work with that same old expression on my face. The expression of a person who'd gotten pushed into a hot mess that sent steam coming out of her eyes. At least now I could vent to the girls and have someone pat me on the back consolingly and have someone else pull me into a hug and have a third someone curse at the person responsible for all this and say to me: "He's not good enough to be a nail on your finger, and before you know it, you'll meet someone who'll appreciate you, get things done and load you off!" I walked into the pharmacy to find all of the above-described scenarios taking place live, and the heroine: Noha! Her thing had fallen apart because her groom found out she was twenty-eight years and three months old when he was looking for someone who was twenty-eight years and two months old. How right he was! What kind of age is twenty-eight and three months?! A totally unromantic age. My blood boiled. This was ridiculous. Even in a situation like this, she couldn't leave me alone! She couldn't even let me enjoy some consolatory pats on the back.

Mrs. Sundus was standing next to her, patting her on the back:

"Don't you upset yourself over this, sweethaaht; before you know it, you'll meet someone who deserves you." (She lowered her voice, not knowing that I was standing right behind her and could still hear her.) "I didn't want to tell you here in front of the girls, but I know a groom who is just too good for anyone else but you!"

"Really, Mrs. Sundus?!"

"Really, I swear! Umm Heba, the woman who sells chickens, told me about him. He's a doctor and he has a clinic and green eyes and dimples!"

For the first time since my thing fell apart, a huge smile appeared on my face. Should I tell her or not? She'd just say that I was eavesdropping. She'd say I was jealous. She'd say I'd always had a thing against her, and it wasn't unlikely that she'd talk to Umm Tarek, the cafeteria lady, and figure out what had happened with Ayman . . . Should I let it go, then? No, that was mean. She was my giiirl, after all.

I heard her whisper to Mrs. Sundus while I was still behind them:

"Whatever you do, don't tell Bride . . . She's the jealous type."

Oh reaaaaaallly?! Well, saddle up, lady, and get ready to meet your fate!

# O. L. D. M. A. I. D.

Oh, how we've laughed! . . . Are we going to be laughing all year, or what?!

Naturally, the letters listed above form a well-known, famous, esteemed, annoying, and incredibly rude description.

Didn't I tell you there was going to be laughter?!

In the Arabic dictionary put together by your ol' uncle Wael El-Sahhah, who is the forty-third descendent of your ol' grandpa Mokhtar El-Sahhah,* the term "old maid" is listed as a synonym for the word "obsolete" and, in another entry, for "the girl who missed the train." . . . May a train pummel anyone who uses the term, amen!

The image that would pop into our heads when we'd hear the phrase "old maid" used to be Zinat Sidky.

A little while later, it became Aisha El-Keilani (both women, by the way, were married in real life).†

Every now and then, you'll find babes past thirty and forty who still haven't gotten married, but you never hear any of them being called old maids. Take for instance—until recently—Laila Eloui. And Latifa, Anoushka.‡ All of them past forty and, yet, have you ever heard anyone call them old maids?! Never!

So if we try to say that the term refers to women who take a while to get married, our definition above wouldn't be accurate. The term is just an insult—nothing more, nothing less. A type of pitiful condescension directed toward a woman you may or may not know . . . It's especially good if you *don't* know the woman.

*A play on the title of one of the earliest comprehensive Arabic dictionaries.
†Egyptian actresses known for their portrayals of older, unmarried characters.
‡Laila Eloui, Latifa, and Anoushka are Egyptian actresses well known for being single. Laila Eloui recently married.

Ohhh yes! Then it's a great description. Something to use when you're joking around, when you're messing about. Something to make people fall about laughing, the same way you laugh when someone's salary gets stolen on the bus. If it happens to you, it's a disaster, but if it happens to someone else . . . well, then that person's stupid and an idiot and a moron and had it coming. The phrase "old maid" is exactly the same. Just look around you—at your family, at your coworkers, at your neighbors. I'm sure you'll find a female relative who's going through this. If you're close, you won't have the heart to call her an old maid. But if you don't know her all that well, well then the phrase glides off your tongue with all the ease in the world.

You use the phrase—I'm sorry to say—in complete ignorance, and you don't realize who it's hurting. And you don't even realize that it *does* hurt.

One time, for example, a girl left me a comment on my blog telling me that what I write about speaks to what she's going through and what a lot of girls are going through. Then some joker jumped in and said: "Well, why don't you gals start an organization and call it The Old Maids Club?!"

Never mind me, I'll talk about me later. But I sat there and I tried to imagine how the girl who'd left me that comment and who'd read what the guy had written must have been feeling. You think she laughed? You think she shrugged it off and forgot all about it?

If you *do* think that, then you have never understood what a girl feels. Because, for almost all women, it's a terrifying issue that kicks in as soon friends and acquaintances start getting engaged and getting married, and when they find themselves taking even just a teeny bit longer to meet someone. As far as I'm concerned, the label has bugged me ever since I was twenty-two. Even hearing it in a movie or on a TV show makes me feel suffocated.

Back to the definition: In the countryside, a girl is considered an old maid if she's still single two years after she gets her *dibloma.*\* In the provinces, the cut-off age used to be twenty-five, and now it's thirty-two to thirty-three. In Cairo and Alexandria, it's thirty-five. And in all cases, the definition covers women who've reached a certain age and have stopped getting suitors. As far as the numbers are concerned, and considering that I don't have a *dibloma*, then I have a little while to go before I carry the label, thank God.

But as for people who throw it around like it's nothing:

If you *do* know that it's hurtful, and you still use it to describe women you know or women you don't know, then it's a catastrophe. And if you *don't* know that the label's hurtful . . . then it's an even bigger catastrophe.

I ask you, please—boycott the label. Because anyone who is incapable of feeling the pain of the person in front of them does not deserve to be a human being.

---

\*A certificate received after completing vocational school or a two-year program, and another instance of confused *b*'s and *p*'s.

# The Ninth

Abeh Ashraf . . . no, of course he's not the groom! What kind
of girl marries her Abeh?! . . . Abeh Ashraf is the new face and
the rising star and the recently recruited player on the national
Searching-for-a-Groom-for-Bride team. Abeh Ashraf is my tante
Rasha's son, and he's only seven years older than I am. But ever
since I was little, I've been calling him Abeh, and he's been buying
me chocolate and giving me Eid money and, sometimes, taking
me out with the rest of the family's innocent little ones to ride the
swings.* I'm not entirely sure why we act like he's twenty or twenty-
five years older than us. Maybe it's because he's levelheaded?
Maybe because he's sensible? Or maybe because he and the statue
of Ramses are two peas in a pod.† The only difference between
them is that Abeh Ashraf is respectable and would *never* stand in
the middle of a public square wearing nothing but a miniskirt like
that Ramses. He's *huge*-huge, but he's still the sweetest and the most
well-behaved person in the world. Which is how my dear mother
got to him so well and was able to milk his naturally occurring
guilt long enough to rope him into joining the national team.

See, the mistake of Abeh Ashraf's life is that it actually
occurred to him to marry someone from outside the family.
The even bigger mistake is that he actually did it. Back then,
the family's leadership council, headed by Mama, got together
and decided that they had to banish Abeh Ashraf from all of the
family residences unless . . . unless . . . The poor thing, because
he's a sweetie, clung onto their "unless" and begged.

*Eid refers to either of the two major Islamic celebrations: Eid-ul-Fitr, which
commemorates the end of Ramadan, or Eid-ul-Adha, which commemorates
Abraham's willingness to sacrifice his son for God.
†Statue of the pharaoh in downtown Cairo.

"I'll do anything to make it up to you, Tante!"

"You should've thought of that before you did what you did, sweetie. Getting married to someone outside the family?! And what exactly are we supposed to do with the girls of the family, then?! Eat them?!"

"It's all fate, Tante."

"No, sweetie, it's grand, premeditated betrayal! Besides, tell me, what does this Nora person have that my daughter, Bride, doesn't?! Huh?"

"But, Tante, Bride has always been like my little sister."

"You just said it yourself. 'Like' . . . which means she *isn't* your sister, which means you can get married! What am I supposed to do now, when she's had her hopes up that you'd propose as soon as you were all settled?"

I tugged at Mama's clothes:

"What are you talking about?! I've never thought that!"

She took me aside and whispered:

"Just be quiet! You don't understand anything. You'll find out soon enough why I'm saying all this. Just stick with me on this one."

So I said fine and I mustered up a look of pain and suffering, and I performed my role in the movie script that was playing out by the book. The poor thing bought the act, felt racked with guilt, and I thought that he was about ready to cry. I freaked out, naturally. He could've drowned the living room! I told you he's the size of the Ramses statue, didn't I?! I leaned over to Mama:

"That's *enough*, Mama."

"I can forgive him on one condition!"

The boy clung to her words like he was drowning and they were the life raft someone had thrown him:

"Anything you want, Tante!"

"You have to find a groom for Bride!"

Look at yooouu and your plans, Mama! This plan, by the
way, will surely one day be part of the How to Hunt Down
a Groom syllabus in high schools (I'm sure we'll get a wise
minister of education in the future who'll realize that girls'
schools in Egypt need a class like this desperately). Anyway, the
boy disappeared that day. Mama *did* say, "Don't show your face
around here unless you've dragged—I mean, brought—along
a groom." And suddenly, after a long period of waiting, Abeh
Ashraf finally showed up, a look of happiness on his face like
he'd scored a goal against El-Negm and was taking El-Ahly to
the Japanese tournament.*

"Tante . . . Tante . . . I've found a groom! I've found a groom!"

"Seriously?! Are you serious, Ashraf?! You're amazing . . . Is
he a friend of yours?"

He answered, hesitating:

"He's . . . no, he's . . . he's not really a friend of mine . . ."

"An acquaintance, then?"

"Not really."

"If he's not a friend and not an acquaintance, what is he?! Did
he come free with a can of tuna from Carrefour?!"†

"No, Tante, he's . . . a friend of a friend's cousin."

"Aha! Well it's obvious how this one's going to turn out. Run
that by me again, sweetie?"

"Tante, it's just that I . . . anytime I start talking to one of my
friends about this and ask them to come propose to my cousin,
they always say: 'Well, why haven't *you* proposed to her?!'"

"Do you see?! Do you see that you've ruined the demand for
these girls?!"

"Not again, Tante. My friend's friend says this groom is
really well behaved and that he's religious and that he has a

---

*A historic game that sent El-Ahly to the 2006 FIFA Club World Cup tournament,
where they proceeded to win the bronze medal.
†A French hypermarket chain, with branches in Cairo and Alexandria.

great personality . . . But all right, Tante. He wanted to visit on Thursday, but I'll tell him not to come."

Mama, panicky as she jumped up and clung to his throat:

"Not to come?! How can he not come?! Of course he must come! He must come! Do you understand?! He must!"

We got everything ready like we had all the other times, except this time Mama made Abeh Ashraf buy the gâteaux and the drinks and the two kilos of chocolate. (Naturally, I didn't object. He had to pay for his mistake.) The groom was supposed to come at seven, so of course we assumed that meant nine or nine thirty (we *were* experts at this thing by now). But he came at seven on the dot. Niiiiice. Good start. He walked in the door, and Abeh Ashraf went to greet him, blocking all air and electricity for me, naturally, so I couldn't see anything. The groom walked into the living room in his shadow. I told myself: Bride, girl, you've got to work this. Wait fifteen, thirty minutes, or say, an hour and fifteen minutes, before you make an entrance. Show him you play hard to get and that you couldn't care less. But Mama, whose dearest wish in life is to cart me out of the family home and ship me off to any other house—the madhouse, even—came and dragged me into the living room.

I stepped into the room and looked around for the groom . . . aaand looked around for the groom . . . There was no groom!

"What's this?! Has he left or something?"

Mama winked at me and Baba gestured with his elbow toward the emptiness on the couch between him and Abeh Ashraf. I moved closer to the couch . . . got reeeaally close . . . until—wham!— Mama ran over to drag me back before I collided with the groom.

"What is this?! Are you telling me the groom's in that space over there?! . . . No way, you guys! You've got to be kidding."

Abeh Ashraf got up and moved to another chair. And what d'ya know?! Apparently, the groom was a tad shy or something and was hiding behind him. I peered at him for a while, paying really close attention . . . He looked like somebody I knew . . . like somebody I knew really well, too . . . It finally hit me and I said it out loud, all happylike:

"Tweety Bird!!!"

The groom got up with a start and Mama pulled me away from him in case he got impulsive or something. But Abeh Ashraf calmed him down and got him to sit down again:

"It's okay, Mr. Mostafa. She's joking, she's just joking."

Well, what was I supposed to do?! He *did* look like Tweety Bird! The big head, the small body, the wide eyes, and that mouth . . . the teeny, crooked little mouth. All that was missing were some yellow feathers and for Hind, Amani's girl, to come pick him up to play with.

I looked at Mama, who was giving me a look of rage that I understood to mean, If you open your mouth, I'm going to set fire to you, and to myself, and to this house. So I swallowed my words and shut up. Besides, so what if he was short?! Were we seriously going to nitpick grooms and make fun of God's creation?! Besides, a ton of tall women marry short men, like that tower of a human being Nicole Kidman, who was married to that midget Tom Cruise. And Tom Cruise and Tweety Bird are cut from the same cloth anyway. It wasn't going to make that much of a difference.

We sat there quietly for a while, and then Mama stood up and got a couple of pieces of gâteaux and put them in front of the groom, along with a cold drink. His highness backed way off and looked at her like she'd brought him rat poison, then shook his head and took the fork and split one of the pieces down the middle. It wasn't just any split, either . . . it was done veeeeeeeerrrryyy carefully, with the expectancy of Nabil El-Halafawy in *The Road to Eilat* when he was tinkering with the

dynamite. He started eating little pieces of the gâteaux, smaller
than the naked eye could see (to match his size and all). After he
was done, he reached out for the drink and took a small sip and
then looked at the cup and then took another small sip and then
looked at the cup. Did he sip for a long time? . . . Sixty-three sips!
I counted them, one sip after another. Then he looked at the glass
one last time, shook his head in self-satisfaction, and put it down,
half empty, half full. During all of this, we were sitting there like
we were watching a movie . . . no, what am I talking about, a
movie?! A cartoon! With sound effects too.

After he was done, he looked at us, and then craned his head up
and looked at the chandelier with disgust, and got up and walked
to the light switch, and jumped and jumped until he could reach it,
and turned the light off. We sat there in the dark, with no idea what
was going on. A few seconds later and the candles that were on
the side tables as decor lit themselves up. I freaked out and jumped
onto Mama's lap, screaming. *Apparently*, our friend the groom had
lit them and moved them to the table in the middle of the room.
By the dancing flames of candlelight I could see the vein in Baba's
forehead begin to quiver. Ahhh, yes. It looked like brother Tweety
would get his share of trips and shoves down the stairwell after all.

Mama, who was still intent on resisting to her last breath, got
up and gave him some chocolate:

"You are so right . . . the atmosphere is much nicer this way."

"No."

"'No,' Mr. Mostafa?"

"No chocolate."

"Oh, right. I bet you're on a diet!"

After he glared at her silently:

"I mean . . . I mean, you must be taking care of your health!"

And she went back to her seat. Suddenly, my cell phone started
ringing, and the groom turned and looked at me:

"Is the cell phone that's ringing in this room?"

"Yeah, it's here."

"Whose is it?"

"It's mine."

That was when the groom jumped up, his shadow reaching the ceiling behind him (oh yeah, I'd never been to the Sound and Light Show* before . . . the light of the candles and the sound of the groom who was screaming at the top of his lungs, that is):

"OHH NO YOU DON'T. ANYTHING BUT THIS!"

Baba, who couldn't take it anymore, got up quickly, turned on the light, and grabbed the groom by his neck:

"Listen up, buddy, I've kept quiet all night because you're my guest and you're in my house. But now, I swear by all things holy, if you don't wise up . . ."

"Me?! Me wise up?! It's *your* family that's all wrong! What is this wastefulness you people are living in?! Chandeliers and TVs and cold drinks and two pieces of gâteaux . . . *Two* pieces of gâteaux, you wasters?! I can go a year without tasting a bit of sugar! And that's not all, either . . . you expect me to marry a woman I'd have to support along with her dependents?!"

"What dependents, you moron?! We're not loading her off with children!"

"Then what would this cell phone be?! It's even worse than children! Caaalls, and meessaaaages, and voice maaaail—am I supposed to spend my money on her or on the cell phone?!"

Mama got up to disentangle them, still insistent on seeing this through:

"Mr. Mostafa, calm down . . . it won't cost you a thing; she pays for it all out of her salary."

"And who said I'm not going to need to take her salary?!"

*Explanatory sound and light show at the Pyramids.

"Whaaaaat?! Oh, you're just here out of greed, then! This is what you come up with, Ashraf?!"

"Out of the way, Tante, I'll handle this . . ."

And Ashraf moved toward the groom, who ducked through his legs, ran out the door, turned to us, and said:

"I could never commit to a woman from a family like this . . . an ignorant, wasteful family!"

And he turned around and left.

Naturally, the neighbors had gathered around at the sound of his voice, and we were scandalized throughout the neighborhood . . . I mean, *he* had turned *us* down, not the other way around!

But no . . . can any show of mine end without someone rolling down the stairs? Of course not! And so it was that we gathered, myself and Mama and Baba, and pushed Abeh Ashraf out the door and tripped him and left him rolling down the stairwell . . . I felt really bad for him. But to be honest, what sustained the most serious damage . . . were the stairs.

# Why Pay More...
## When You Can Pay Less?

That darling little saying affects the lives of all Egyptians, directly and indirectly. It is, really, the second most important thing we believe in after God, and it's implemented in a ton of ways throughout our daily lives, and through two particular models: the saver model and the cheapskate model. (Of course, there's another saying that goes: why work more when you can work less?! A popular one among government employees and Zamalek players . . . but that's not the issue right now.)

Generally speaking, the Egyptian populace is one of planet Earth's most scheming and thrifty peoples (who just turned on the television?). The upstanding Egyptian citizen has ways of saving money that should be taught in economics programs in all corners of the civilized world. Starting with school books that are passed down from the oldest kid to the one after to the one after. Even if the curricula change . . . So what?! It's all knowledge, isn't it?! To the shoes that make the same rounds as the school uniforms, and the going out clothes, and the staying at home clothes, to the backpacks, and even down to the underwear whose role in the national realm goes beyond the usual and extends to its being used in kitchens to carry hot pots and to wipe floors and to stuff under the pantries' broken legs so that they don't wobble.

Now the Egyptian woman has a proactive and influential role in this national mission, starting with her raising chickens and ducks on the roof, to the pickles and jam that she makes with her own hands, down to her mighty national role of gathering empty tomato sauce jars and old newspapers and plastic bags and storing them under the beds. You'll ask her:

"But why?!" And she'll say: "And why not?! They might be useful some day!"

All of these things are great and are part of a national, countrywide heritage that brings pride to every citizen who lives on Egypt's soil, drinks from its Nile, and sings to its grandeur. But what we're talking about now isn't savers . . . it's cheapskates. Specifically when it comes to what?! . . . Bravo! Marriage! (What else am I always thinking of?!)

Marriages in general, and living-room marriages specifically, get treated by everyone like they're business transactions.

The groom will think: Well, since I don't really know her, and she doesn't know me, then it's only smart to get through the transaction with the smallest possible amount of incurred losses.

And the bride will think: I don't love him, and I couldn't care less about him, really. He needs to just pay up and haul me off.

He'll act like a weasel and she'll try to take him for all he's got, and the tug-of-war begins. Either the rope tears down the middle or they reach common ground and see the thing through to a happy ending. Considering that I am (of course!) on the girls' side of all this, and considering my wiiiiide range of experiences with grooms, here are a bunch of situations a girl can use to figure out if his highness, her future groom, has tight-fisted weasel tendencies and cheapskate blood running through his veins. Afterward, she must act accordingly. And all those seeking damages must appeal to the courts.

For example:

- The first time he visits your apartment, he walks in empty-handed. (Because how does he know it's going to work out? Is he supposed to just waste money on gâteaux for nothing?!)

- You talk about the wedding jewelry (that is, if he's willing to buy wedding jewelry in the first place), and he says, "Oh, no, no. Your jewelry is ready already! I had it brought in from the Emirates special. They cheat you on gold here, and I want you to have only the best." (Needless to say, he's bought it from the jewelers' behind the gas station near their house. Which is much better than taking you to pick out the jewelry yourself and ending up paying a fortune.)
- If God gets you through the jewelry talk safe and sound, and you're able to get the jewelry you want, and you go ahead and get engaged, you find him insisting, with unshakeable determination, that you don't go out together. He says, "It's forbidden in our religion! We aren't legally married yet and God wouldn't be happy with it." (Naturally, you realize that he's trying to save the money he'd spend on the outings . . . because the boy doesn't even know what prayer looks like.)
- If God gives you the strength to force him to go out, he says: "What do you want fancy restaurants and all that nonsense for?! What's wrong with Cook Door?"*
- And if you compromise and go to Cook Door with him, he steals your fries. And, when you leave, it won't be all that surprising if he reaches for the rest of the sandwich in your doggie bag. Then he says: "Like that proverb says, I want to eat your food so I can chase you for a lifetime!"†
- He "coincidentally" hits rough patches every holiday season: On the Prophet's birthday, his wallet gets stolen. On the first of Ramadan, he gets a pay cut. In

---

*Inexpensive fast-food restaurant.
†Sharing food is considered to be pivotal in bonding people.

the middle of Shaaban, he has appendicitis. And on the 28th of Rajab, his mother's eyebrow hurts.*

- If you try to milk any possible thing out of the holidays, and if you whine and moan, and if you ask him straight out to buy you some clothes for the small Eid, he says: "But this holiday is about *kahk*,[†] not clothes!" And on the big Eid, he says, "But this holiday is about meat! Didn't you buy mutton this season?!"

- Every day you find him mooching off your family's lunch (mooch, to mooch, for he is a mooch). And he says: "I just want to cement my relationship with my in-laws, and cementing only works if you break some bread together!"

- And when you tell him that you, too, would like to cement your relationship with your in-laws, he says: "No, sweetie. Mama cooks with a lot of butter, and I don't want you to get fat."

- You go pick out the furniture and he chooses the smallest fridge and the smallest washing machine. If he could get a crippled-looking stove with one eye, he'd be all for it.

- When you're picking out the bedroom furniture; if your family's paying for the room, then he chooses the king-sized bed. If *he's* paying, then he chooses the smallest bed on the market. And if you object, he says: "I don't want a big bed, because I always want you close, in my arms."

*The middle of Shaaban commemorates the changing of the Qibla—the direction toward which Muslims pray—from Jerusalem to Mecca. The 28th of Rajab commemorates al-'Isrā' wal-Mi'rāǧ, the Prophet Muhammed's journey to Jerusalem and ascencion to Heaven.
†Type of cookies traditionally prepared and eaten in celebration of Eid.

- He refuses to have ceramic tiles put in, and goes for linoleum . . . so you don't slip.
- He refuses to buy rugs and says: "Why would I want to hide the ceramic tiles?!" (That your dad bought.)
- He refuses to buy chandeliers and says: "I don't like that type of lighting. Why don't we go with neon?"
- You look for reception halls for the wedding and he says: "Let's do this Islamic-style. Who needs a DJ or a band?!" (I thought we already said you don't know what praying looks like?!)

So it's imperative that you're patient and that you wake up and see what's really going on. It's a battle, girlfriend. Fight or flight. He pulls a fast one, you block him. He goes up, you bring him down. Either you fight him on everything and break the whole thing up, or you let slide whatever you want to let slide so that the boat can keep sailing on its way and you can get through the marriage process okay.

But I don't want you to worry. Because she who has the last laugh, laughs the best. At the end of the day, you're going to come out on top, and you'll take out every little thing that happened to you on him when you hold all the cards in your hand and implement your sacred duty as the minister of economics and expenditures in your household. Then he won't even have the option to spend more . . . or spend less.

# The Tenth

Emad the Magnificent is back in town! No, no, he wasn't on tour with the circus or anything. It's true that "the Magnificent" is his nickname, but it's a description too. Emad is *the* boy next door, as is good and fitting for him to be. Not just as far as I'm concerned, but as far as swarms of girls in our neighborhood and surrounding areas are concerned, too (check your local listings for accurate times).

The sentence "Emad the Magnificent is back in town" could strike you as no big deal. As a "so what?" . . . What do you mean, "so what"?! The whole neighborhood went topsy-turvy! Balconies were cleaned and rugs were beaten and girls were primped. Mrs. Afaf, who owns the beauty salon at the end of the block, bought her daughters three new sets of gold, inspired by that one sentence: "Emad the Magnificent is back in town."

The boy is magnificent . . . truly magnificent. Not just as far as his looks are concerned, but his personality too. Despite the fact that all of the neighborhood girls have bent over backwards trying to get him to send a single look or smile their way, he's always been super, super polite. He's never leered at one of us . . . *them* . . . I mean, one of *them* . . . And he's never given any of us . . . dang it . . . I mean, *them* . . . the time of day. That's what's made this into such a big deal in our heads, and made the competition fiercer than ever before.

The day the Great Disaster befell us and we found out he was going off to London, our innocent virginal hearts (nice one, eh?!) were broken. Even though we knew exactly where to track him down (London, behind Big Ben, one block to the left, and one block to the right), our hearts were still shattered into a million

pieces. Ever since then, every so often, one of us will look toward
the window of his room, sigh, and say, "Ahhh, the good ol' days!"

That's why our very souls were invigorated when we heard
that he'd come back. And that's why the tree of hope started
blooming again after its branches had shriveled inside of our
hearts (. . . where do I come up with this stuff?!). The whole
neighborhood was green, and girls' faces changed from being
so grouchy they'd stop a man dead in his tracks—other girls'
faces, not mine, of course—to smiling and happy again.
Especially since we found out that the reason he was back was
that his dear mother swore up and down that he had to come
back and get married so that she could stop worrying about
him. Ever since then, girls have left anything and everything
they had to do behind and have camped out by their windows
or on their balconies or even on the roof, in case Emad came
out and looked around and said, "Now *she's* the one I've been
looking for!" That way, a girl would get a groom *and* a free trip
to London.

Now I, of course, wasn't playing that game at all. So, yes, it
was true that I took a week off work and stayed home . . . but
that's normal. It happens. And it was also true that I was
spending all day on the balcony, but that was becaaauuse . . . I
just couldn't let the plants on the neighbor's balcony underneath
us die. I'd stand around a mere two or three hours watering
them (Yes, two or three hours. I was watering the plants using
the dripping technique so that they wouldn't drown, okay?). As
soon as he'd look out his window, every girl would drop whatever
was in her hands and strike a pose under some form of lighting
that would allow him to see her properly. He'd move his head
around and flash a panoramic smile that would include all of us
and that would, at the same time, make every girl feel that it was
for her and for her alone.

During his first week back, his family's apartment turned into a pilgrimage site. Someone would show up to "borrow an egg" and someone would drop by to ask about the Hagga's health and someone would swing by with some rice pudding. Except for me, of course. The only time I dropped by, my shirt had flown off our clothesline and landed on theirs. True, their clothesline was across from ours and was about ten meters away, but how was I supposed to control the wind?! You know how strong it gets in August . . .

I went to their apartment and his mom gave me this huuuu-uge smile. I got super happy, but then I told myself: Don't be silly, Bri-Bri. She probably does this with everyone. Then she grabbed me and showered me with kisses. To be honest, I welled up a little. I'd never been kissed before. Even Mama won't kiss me. And then—wham!—she brought out some chocolate and handed it to me. All that was missing was for her to give me a quarter and tell me to run off and buy myself some candy. Calm down, Bri-Bri. This could just be how she expresses emotion. She's luring you in with the chocolate and then she'll start talking . . . I waited . . . nothing. I waited some more . . . absolutely nothing. Then the woman started looking concerned, so she figured she'd do something to stabilize the situation and went and got another piece of chocolate and handed it to me, her thinking being that I was a pig and needed more than the one piece (which was, to tell you the truth, very small).

I left, confused. What was the meaning of what had happened? I figured I had nothing to lose, and so I trekked around, gathering stuff to eat and drink, grabbed my pillow, and camped out on the balcony, my eyes on his window. I wasn't about to go to sleep without figuring out what exactly was going on. And God didn't let me down either. Only a few minutes had gone by when Emad popped out of the window and visually swept

the audience in the windows and balconies until he spotted me.
Then he gave me a big smile and said:

"Pssst . . . pssst."

(Oh YAY! My very first psssting!)

"Yes?"

"Tell your dad that Mama and I are coming to visit you today."

BAM . . . BAM . . . BOOM . . . That would be the sound of girls
fainting and collapsing and of windows being slammed shut and
of the potted plant that had been hurled at the wall right next to
my head. I was oblivious to everything going on around me. Even
when that chick Asmaa threw herself off the balcony and people
gathered around . . . diiiidn't even glance at her. (Are you trying
to tell me that a woman who wants to die throws herself off a first-
floor balcony?! What kind of nauseating child's play is that?!)

I shut the balcony doors and went back inside.

"Mama! Mama! Congratulate me! After all the black disasters
that I've been through . . . God is finally rewarding my patience!
Emad and his mother are coming to make a proposal today!"

"So the plant-watering and the shirts-that-fly-through-the-air
thing worked?!"

"What're you talking about, Mama?! I have no idea what
you mean!"

"Yeah, yeah. At least we know that Emad's one of our own.
Let's just wait and see how all of this ends."

So he came with his mom that night to a living-room
gathering completely unparalleled in the entire history of
my marital meetings. A calm gathering it was . . . a classy
gathering . . . Everyone taaaalked calmly and everyone smiiiiled
calmly. Now *this* was a romantic marital atmosphere all right.
All that was missing was for Omar Khairat to play us some
background piano,* a little romantic ditty from *The Night of*

*Egyptian classical pianist.

*Fatma's Incarceration,* say. A short while after we started talking, his mother gave my mother a look that I understood when I saw them get up and take Baba with them out of the room, leaving us alone.

God, could it get more awkward?! So it's true that I was ready to die of happiness, especially since this was the first time I'd gone past the first-hour mark and reached the "sitting alone together" stage . . . Oh, but it was so awkward! Even he looked like he was embarrassed and uncomfortable, his eyes on the floor. Every time I looked up at him, he'd look up at the same time, and then we'd both look right back at the floor. Okay, so I'M shy, I thought, but c'mon, YOU live in Europe. Take some initiative and say something! . . . You guys, I just really want someone to talk to me lovingly . . . As if he'd heard what was going through my head, he gathered up his courage, looked up, and started talking:

"Bride . . . I . . ."

And all of a sudden, his cell phone rang. (Good God, what kind of timing was this?!) He looked at the phone really intently, answered the call, and spoke in English the whole time:

"Yeah . . . yeah, how are you? Are the lab results out yet? . . . What happened? . . . Well, is he mine or John's? . . . He's mine . . . well, thank God . . . Okay, bye."

He turned off his cell phone, smiling broadly. I figured I should ask him what had happened, as moral support and all:

"You look happy . . . What's going on? Good news?"

"Very!"

"I must be your good luck charm, then! Who were you talking to?"

"That was Margaret."

"Margaret?! . . . Who's Margaret? A work friend?"

"No . . . Margaret's my wife."

I jumped up like I'd been stung by a scorpion:

"YOUR WIFE?! What do you mean, YOUR WIFE?! . . . You're MARRIED?"

"I . . . I thought Mama had told you guys about my situation."

"What situation?! And if you're married, what the heck are you visiting us for?!"

"Well, I'm sure you understand that a guy who goes to Europe has to get citizenship, and so he has to marry a woman who has it. It's the only option, really."

I calmed down a little bit and sat down . . . still angry, though . . . Maybe he really did have no other option.

"I *could* choose to make a sacrifice and try to overlook this . . . since it's just a marriage of convenience."

"You see . . . we . . . it's not really a marriage of convenience. To be honest, we ended up falling in love, and our marriage isn't just a thing on paper anymore."

I jumped up again:

"Then WHY, you idiot, are you here right now?!"

"It's Mama who insists on marrying me off to someone from here so that I can visit regularly and not stay away from her too long!"

"Ahhhh . . . you mean, your mom wants to use me as a lasso to rope in the bull—that would be your highness—so that it doesn't stray too far."

"Please, Miss . . . there's no reason to talk like that."

"Talk?! . . . What talk?! Oh, it's going to turn into action now, buddy!"

Then I lunged, trying to get at his neck. Mama and Baba and his precious mother came running in when they heard the screams so that they could tear us apart. Mama was trying to gain control of the situation before I went ahead and whacked him.

"What is going on, Bride?! Have you lost your mind?!"

"Lost my mind?! I swear to God I have every right to lose my mind . . . Enough! I'm tired! I'm so tired! . . . COME HERE

SO I CAN TAKE EVERYTHING I'VE BEEN THROUGH OUT ON YOUR SORRY BEHIND."

"Calm down! Calm down and talk to me . . . What is going on?!"

"His highness here!"

"What about him?"

"He's MARRIED."

His mother screamed.

"On paper . . . on paper, I swear. For the citizenship."

"Oh no, lady. Ask your son . . . he says he *loves* her!"

Baba was watching the guy and looked like he wanted to say something, when I said:

"Leave this to me, Baba . . . Mr. Emad . . . GET OUT! We don't have any girls who want to get married here."

He gave us a look like we had passed up the opportunity of a lifetime, took his mother, and headed toward the door. I called out after him:

"Wait! Before you leave, and so I can record this whole thing down in the history books properly . . . what's going on with the lab tests and the 'Is he mine or John's' business?"

"Why do you want to know?"

"I just do, okay?! Satisfy my curiosity to make up for what you did to me."

"Well . . . well, Margaret and I fought about three months ago, and she went back to her old boyfriend, and then we got back together, and now she's pregnant. So we had to run some tests to figure out if it's mine or John's. There was no way I was going back to her if the kid wasn't mine."

Then Baba was the one screaming:

"Oh, what a PLAAAAYYEER YOU ARE! Tell me, Mr. Emad, your nickname's 'the Magnificent,' isn't that right?!"

"Yes."

"No other nicknames you're hiding from us?!"

"No. None."

"Are you sure?!"

His highness stood there, thinking for a little bit, and then it looked like he understood what Baba was trying to say.

He turned around, and what d'ya know?! He was *offended*:

"Let's go, Mama. This family is not for us!"

His precious mother said:

"We'll find another family, sweetheart. There are a ton of girls around."

Exactly . . . that is the exact problem . . . there are a tooooooooooooooooooooooooooooooooooon of girls around.

God help us all.

# That Noha Chick Is Engaged! . . . Whhhhhhyyyy?!

The . . . news . . . hit . . . us . . . LIKE LIGHTENING HAD
STRUCK!!!!!

That *sneak*! Didn't say a single word! We had no idea it was
happening! No news from her whatsoever. And then what?! We
went home one day, came back the next, found her standing
in the middle of the pharmacy, and—bam!—she stuck up her
hand, the ring shining on her finger.

"Aren't you going to congratulate me, you guys?! I'm engaged!"

The pharmacy, which had been bustling, came to a complete
and sudden halt. Like we'd been watching a tape and it
had frozen and needed to be cleaned to start playing again.
Everything came to a standstill. Even the patients at the counter
stood there and stared, even though they had no idea what was
going on. It was like they were thinking: Is it *really* possible for
one of *them* to be engaged?! We all turned toward her slowly,
glaring, and the girl took a couple of steps back, ready to make
a run for it. All of a sudden, some incredibly loud trilling rang
out, originating from—naturally—Mrs. Sundus. *She* didn't
have anything to lose, after all. After Mrs. Sundus was off and
going, and had pulled the girl into a hug, we glanced at each
other, figuring we wouldn't look too great if we didn't go over to
say congratulations. So we each pulled a smile out of the purse
that we carry for occasions like these—nice image there, huh?!
Isn't that what you call an extended metaphor? Like they use
in classical rhetoric?—sucked it up like we were being force-fed
twelve kilos of lemons, and congratulated her on the ever-so-
happy occasion. Happy my foot . . .

The girl *kept on putting her hand* in our faces like she was itching
to stick her finger right into our eyes. Enough already, lady,
enough—we've seen the ring. This was too much; she wasn't the
first person in the world to be engaged. Naturally, after the wave
of congratulations (issued straight from the heart, of course) had
passed, our day continued on like a scene from a movie with
our dearly departed colleague Charlie Chaplin. Compleeeetely
silent, in other words. The only sounds were Noha whispering
things to Mrs. Sundus and the two of them giggling back and
forth. Yep, the two were total BFFs now, since they were just like
each other because each one had a man and all.

As for the rest of the pharmacy . . . God protect you. This
one girl, Samah, kept getting up and standing in front of the
window. We'd ask her what was wrong and she'd say: "I feel like
I'm suffocating . . . I'm suffocating! I can't breathe!" Another
girl, Nevine, was sympathizing—for the first time in the history
of the Ministry of Health—with the patients, and handling their
requests gently . . . I'm guessing she figured that all the patients'
curses directed at her when she'd thrown their prescriptions
in their faces were ruining things for her. So she decided she'd
change the game plan and stick with a 4-2-4 player arrangement
instead, so that God would throw her a bone.* Now Samar had us
*really* worried. Every few minutes, she'd walk toward the rat poison
that was in the supply closet and look at it really strangely. That's
what had us monitoring her all day, and pulling her away from
her cup of tea and the cup Noha was drinking from. We wouldn't
relax until she left the poison alone and started playing with a pair
of scissors. Scissors were easy. She'd hurt something we could sew
back up, but what were we supposed to do with poison?!

As far as I was concerned, I was happy. Yeah, that's right.
Happy. What of it?! It's true the girl was a sneak and a show-

*One possible arrangement of players on a soccer field.

off and a snob and a weasel, but she was a fellow soldier of strife. It's true that I'd grown to consider any engagement or marriage on the face of the planet a personal insult to my being, but it was okay. Maybe she was just standing at the beginning of the line and everyone else would follow. It's true that we said the same thing when Mrs. Sundus got married four years ago . . . but maybe someone would get married every four years . . . So we'd need . . . 4 x 13 . . . which is . . . 52 years until we'd load off all the girls in the pharmacy. But there you go . . . there was still hope.

As the longest day in history passed, she'd throw us a bit of information every so often:

"Well, Hossam . . ." (The name of the unluckiest schmuck in the world.)

"Well, in his hospital . . ." (Which meant that he was a doctor.)

"Well, his mother, God rest her soul . . ." (*And* you don't have a mother-in-law, either?! You lucky cow.)

Suddenly, at the end of the day, she turned to us, and with all the smugness in the world, said:

"Please excuse me, everyone. Hossam is about to pick me up in his car . . ."

A surreptitious look here and there, three to four whispering voices, and pursed lips occurred across the pharmacy. Then she finished the sentence:

"Why don't you come with us, Mrs. Sundus? We'll drive you home."

Well of course. She was the only one who could be trusted! The rest of us were dangerous around her little precious. To be honest, she was right. If I'd heard about this sooner, I would've sent the guy off to Benghazi to marry Ayman's sister-in-law. (I hope you're doing well, Ayman, and may God return you safe and sound to your family!)

So her highness ran off, and we took off after her, tripping on the stairs and knocking over everything in our way: patients, staff members, even the plastic trees in front of the manager's office. All so we could get there in time to watch her and the little precious in his car.

The guy wasn't too bad looking . . . I mean, you could work with him. It's true that he was as skinny as a pencil, and every few seconds he'd have to catch his pants before they fell off of him, and it was obvious that his ears either had personal vendettas against each other or respected his head so very much they were standing on guard in a hideous way. But it was God's creation. And true, he was wearing gallon-bottle, not just Coke-bottle, glasses, and they were so big they weren't just there for his eyes, but were helping out his eyebrows and his cheeks, too. But he was a man. And how many women can actually find a good man these days? So the car wasn't a 16er—that would be a 4x4; I'm all about shortening things but it was still a classy affair: a red 128 Peugeot, circa 1979. The girl sat next to him like she was at the Prophet's birthday fair with the emcee's son,* and gave us a look brimming with rage and condescension, and Mrs. Sundus got in behind her. I hope you run into your husband on the way so he can make your life a living hell! It's such a horrible feeling when someone the same age as you and who's gone through the same trials as you and who even works in the same place as you and who's shared the thick and thin with you suddenly pulls an act of grand betrayal like this . . . it really hurts.

When I got home and told Mama all about it, she looked at the phone thoughtfully, and reached out and started dialing a number I know all too well . . . Auntie-Body's number. I stopped

---

*Among the Egyptian working classes, street fairs are a popular way to celebrate the Prophet Muhammed's birthday, and commemorate the lives of Muslim holy men and women.

her before she could finish dialing and we looked right at each other, and I said, with depth and intensity:

"No, Mama, no! . . . Don't make me sink that low!"

Then I grabbed the phonebook:

"What's Uncle Disco's number, again?"

# Thirties Girl

A lot of people out there think that girls are asking for it, that if they had just settled for the bare minimum, Egypt wouldn't be teeming with girls stuck in a late-marriage rut right now. Even though, as you may have noticed, I never talk about finances in my living room-ian stories and adventures—because what's important to me has never been money and because the suitors who come visit know who they're meeting and know what our financial situation is like (nothing too great or anything)—it's still never happened that we've gotten a proposal from someone who was completely broke, and we've never turned anyone down because they didn't have enough money, either. It's actually the opposite—Baba is the understanding type. The crisis, as far as I'm concerned, doesn't have anything to do with money. It has to do with personality and manners and upbringing, and it's about finding a human being I can depend on when I need to. But there are *still* people out there who will insist that it's totally and completely the girl's fault, hers and her family's, for asking too much of a groom, for paralyzing him, and for destroying all his ambitions and his dreams of finding someone to commit to. They'll insist that we have to gather up girls and their families everywhere and beat them to death with clogs, because *they're* the reason guys feel defeated and *they're* the reason their futures are destroyed. I'm not denying, at all, that some people out there do ask for too much and some people do make completely unreasonable demands, but these days there's a growing number of people who will accept anything just so they can get it over with and get rid of that back-crippling load known as "daughters."

Never mind that issue. On to the next: the thirties. And how little ye know of the thirties! One theory says that, in your thirties, you gather up the losers and you get it over with already . . . a man's a man, after all. You pop out a couple of kids and you help them with their homework, and he spends the rest of his life sitting at the coffee shop or in a café or on the Internet. And they all live happily ever after—the end.

Those holding to the opposing theory retort: "You mean I fast, and I fast, and then I feast on a schmuck?! I had my choice of better men and I turned them down. And you supported it! And this way, I'm just going to spend the rest of my life being miserable. And if I'm going to be miserable, I might as well be miserable on my own terms . . . watching the soaps on Channel 1 instead of the Zamalek game, sleeping at night without someone who'll hog the covers, or who'll eat all the chicken and leave the wings for me . . . Or am I supposed to settle for a guy who'll treat me that way just so I can escape blame, save myself from being called a you-know-what?!" And so the struggle begins. "Should I wait and trust that God will reward me in the end? Or should I just accept that this is what my luck is like and call it a day?"

If anyone thinks that women in their thirties nowadays are like women in their thirties a long time ago . . . desperate . . . then they're wrong. A thirties girl has spent at least seven or eight years on her own. Loneliness hurts, it's true, but she got used to it after a while, made her peace with it, even. So she's not about to run toward any groom just because she's alone. A thirties girl has been employed for seven or eight years, seen all sorts of people, understood all sorts of people. It's not as easy as it used to be to pull one over on her with some lines and a bottle of perfume, or a red rose. A thirties girl doesn't care so much anymore about marrying someone who'll look at her with googly eyes all day, who'll spend an hour primping his hair, and she's not going to faint when she smells the cologne he's bathed in either. A thirties girl has seen a lot of people get married and a lot of people get divorced. It has given her experience, a certain outlook on things, and it's made her demand things of a future husband that go beyond the dreams of a girl in her twenties who wants nothing more than to put on a veil, sit in a reception hall, and spend her honeymoon in Marina,* and who doesn't think much about marriage beyond that. A thirties girl has held down jobs, has made money, and she doesn't need a man to support her financially anymore, so it's not likely that she'll be impressed with an apartment or jewelry or a car. The thirties girl looks for personality before she looks for looks. She looks at a person's family before she looks at an individual. She looks for stability before she looks for social status or money. Anyone who thinks thirties girls are desperate and will settle for anything needs to read this over and think again.

A lot of people will say: "Well, then, clearly you don't want to get married at all!" And I'll say: "That isn't what most women out there want. But it's out there, and it's going strong, so consider yourself warned."

*A popular beach resort on Egypt's north coast.

# In the End

There is no end yet. The book may be finished, but the story isn't. A lot of women and I are still looking for a husband: not just as a means of support or protection, but as a person to share our lives and our happiness and our sadness with. A person who will understand us and who we'll understand. Who'll respect us and who we'll respect. A person we can feel genuinely safe with. And until God wills it and every girl out there finds her other half, we'll keep watching and living and running into stories and situations that deserve to be told. And I, I will keep voicing my right, and I won't be embarrassed if anyone hears me say it: "I want to get married!"

Bride

# A Final Word

When I enrolled in pharmacy school a few years ago, I was forced to put my literary leanings aside, and after I graduated, I, like many other girls, entered a whirlwind of grooms and proposals and living-room meetings. Throughout it all, I was confronted with a number of situations and experiences that I kept to myself. When I looked for a way to communicate these experiences and my feelings, I found myself welcomed in cyberspace. So I set up my blog around a year and a half ago, and I titled it I Want to Get Married! In it, I sarcastically presented the experiences and situations that I had been through. A short while later, the blog became famous and its readership spread so widely I was amazed. Many people considered it to be one of the best blogs in the Arabic language, an honor I can only hope my blog deserves. Despite this, however, I continued to dream that my writing would be freed from the restrictions of cyberspace and released into the expanse of the world. Now, my dream has come true and I Want to Get Married! has been transformed into the book you are holding. My only hope is that it has earned your pleasure, and that it has brought you closer, if only by a single step, to the thoughts of an Egyptian girl trying hard to perform the role her society has allotted her . . . and until salvation arrives, she will keep saying it, loudly or quietly, or in a whisper: "I want to get married."

Ghada Abdel Aal
(honors marital life . . . and helps buy the furniture)

CPSIA information can be obtained
at www.ICGtesting.com
Printed in the USA
FFOW02n2224050817
38534FF